John Wall: The Inspiring Story of One of Basketball's Fastest Point Guards

An Unauthorized Biography

By: Clayton Geoffreys

Table of Contents

Foreword

Since entering the league as the first overall pick of the 2010 NBA Draft, John Wall has electrified the nation's capital. A flashy point guard armed with impressive ball handling abilities and speed, John Wall has emerged to become one of the top ten point guards in the NBA today. This never came as much of a surprise, as Wall displayed flashes of brilliance as early as his rookie season in the NBA, when he became the third youngest player to record a triple-double in NBA history. His explosive nature has enabled him to take on the role of leading the Washington Wizards to win their first playoff series in six years when they eliminated the Chicago Bulls in five games in the 2014 NBA Playoffs. Since that time, the Wizards returned to the playoffs in 2015 and 2017. In many regards, the Wizards have redirected the course of their franchise with the pairing of John Wall and Bradley Beal in their backcourt. Wall's ascension in the NBA comes at a prime time as quick and dynamic point guards have become a staple of several NBA teams such as the Golden State Warriors, Oklahoma City Thunder, and Boston Celtics. The game has fundamentally shifted towards a faster style of play, which will continue to align well with John Wall's strengths. Thank you for purchasing *John Wall: The Inspiring Story of One of Basketball's Fastest Point Guards*. In this unauthorized biography, we will learn John's incredible life story and impact on the game of basketball. Hope you enjoy and if you do, please do not forget to leave a review! Also, check out my website at claytongeoffreys.com to join my exclusive list where I let you know about my latest books and give you goodies!

Cheers,

Clayton Geoffreys

Visit me at www.claytongeoffreys.com

Introduction

What makes an NBA player a star? Is it the spectacular highlights or flashy dunks? Maybe it is the endorsements paid by global companies. How about putting up impressive numbers such as points, rebounds, or assists? Could that be it? Maybe it is the impact they have on the game of basketball.

The answer is none of the above. In the narrative-driven world of sports journalism, an NBA star is defined by whether he wins or loses. Dallas Mavericks star Dirk Nowitzki was widely panned as a choker when the Mavericks collapsed in the 2007 first round, but today, he is revered as an all-time great after winning the 2011 title. LeBron James was castigated for his failures in the 2011 Finals. But today, he is respected after winning two straight rings and after delivering the first title to the Cleveland Cavaliers. More often than not, the justifications or excuses for why a winner won or a loser lost are made up in hindsight as opposed to calm analysis.

Even LeBron James, who came into the league in 2003 as the next face of the NBA, was marketed as the man that would carry the league into the future. Before winning his first NBA title in 2012 and despite arguably playing at a level a cut above the rest of the NBA, LeBron was criticized for his lack of a championship ring and for struggling in his Finals appearances.

But when James finally won the NBA title he rightfully deserved, he was immediately catapulted to a level of stardom unseen since the peak of Kobe Bryant. He was even put on a pedestal high enough to challenge all-time greats such as Michael Jordan, Magic Johnson, and Larry Bird. That was what winning a championship did to LeBron. By becoming a winner, he was immortalized.

The same could also be said about Kevin Durant. KD came into the NBA with a lot of expectations on his slender shoulders because of his rare ability to score the basketball. He has since become a four-time scoring leader and is arguably the best scorer in basketball since Michael Jordan. However, he continuously failed to win a title with the Oklahoma City Thunder and was criticized because of his inability to become a champion. Criticisms further erupted when he moved to an already dominant Golden State Warriors. But the talks silenced when he defeated LeBron's Cleveland Cavaliers in the 2017 NBA Finals to finally cement himself as a once-in-a-generation superstar.

So what will it be for Washington Wizards point guard John Wall? Ever since he burst onto the high school scene back in 2008-2009, Wall was known more for his athleticism and dance moves than for playing winning basketball. But despite such impressions, Wall has imparted toughness and a new, more mature culture to a Wizards team once filled with knuckleheads and a shameless tradition of losing.

Since the fall of the peak years of Gilbert Arenas, Caron Butler, and Antawn Jamison in the middle of the 2000 decade, the Wizards were never really competitive as a group. They have since struggled with players that had attitude problems and guys that cared more about the money and fame instead of the wins. However, Washington's record has improved every year since Wall burst onto the scene of the NBA.

John Wall not only gave the Wizards the go-to guy they sorely needed, but he also provided them the spark that ensured Washington of a hopeful future led by a young and growing star. With his athleticism, Wall ran opposing teams down to the ground on his best days. And when he was not scoring for the Wizards, he made it a point to set teammates up for easy baskets on the break or during set plays.

On top of all of his abilities to spark the offense, John Wall came into Washington as a capable defender for the Wizards. With all those skills and abilities, Wall was the ultimate player that any team would choose to build on for their future given his youth and potential. Nevertheless, it took time for Wall to finally mature into a leader that could take his team to greater heights.

It would take until the 2013-2014 season for the Wizards to make the playoffs for the first time since 2008. After defeating the Chicago Bulls in 5 games, the Wizards were headed to the second round for the first time since 2005 and had a very realistic chance to make the Eastern Conference Finals. While John Wall's supporting cast has improved since his rookie year, it has been his leadership and poise that has helped take the Wizards to where they are today.

The Washington Wizards would make the playoffs the next season. They had developed into one of the fastest-rising teams in the whole league. From a team of hard-headed yet talented individuals, it was Wall's leadership and development that led to the overall growth of the Washington Wizards. With the maturity needed from a franchise player, John Wall had become one of the best point guards in the NBA and will continue to develop while his team needs him to.

Along with John Wall's development came the rise of his backcourt teammate Bradley Beal. While the Washington Wizards had originally planned for Wall and Beal to be the backcourt of the future for the franchise, things did not start out well. Beal struggled to translate his game to the NBA level and was strictly a catch-and-shoot player that struggled to get shots. Meanwhile, John Wall never thought highly of his backcourt teammate and openly criticized Beal when the latter received a lucrative extension with the Washington Wizards despite not putting up enough numbers to become an All-Star or contributing enough to the team's overall success.

However, Bradley Beal has since developed into a player worthy of being called one of the best shooting guards in the league. Along with a new system implemented by head coach Scott Brooks during the 2016-17 season, John Wall has flourished in the backcourt with Beal. The two have since become one of the top backcourt duos in the entire NBA and have gelled well together to turn the Wizards into an upstart team that could give a scare to any team in the Eastern Conference. Beal's rise not only made the Wizards a better team but also helped John Wall improve his performance and numbers across the board to become a sure 20-10 double-double threat at the point guard position.

Formerly seen as a one-man star trying to carry the Wizards on his own, John Wall has become an elite point guard not only because of his hard work and the new system but also because of the rise of his backcourt partner, who has helped ease the burden off him. His supporting cast has also risen to the challenge. Otto Porter and Markieff Morris have both developed into exceptional players that made the shots that John Wall opened up for them and have delivered during the times when neither of the Wizards' backcourt stars was in their best form.

Now, what makes an NBA star? It is the ability to make his teammates better through example and by making things easier for them on the floor. John Wall has done that and continues his journey to become an elite superstar in the league and into one of the most feared leaders and point guards not just in today's NBA but in the history of the sport as well.

Chapter 1: Childhood and Early Life

Johnathan Hildred Wall, Jr. was born on September 6, 1990, to Frances Pully and John Wall, Sr. in Raleigh, North Carolina. Like many NBA players, Wall had a rough childhood. His father was in jail for armed robbery and had earlier served a charge for second-degree murder – all before Wall was eight. Wall frequently visited his father in prison on the weekends, which was an event that he looked forward to every week. His mother would take him and his younger sister, Cierra, to visit their father. These visits lasted for two hours, and each time, they would try to resemble a family gathering as much as possible. It was probably for John's best that he never learned what his father had done until just before he entered the NBA at the age of 19.

His father did love the young John, and he would give his son superhero pictures or other crafts that he made in prison. For example, Wall was sent a handmade card on his fifth birthday. It was a detailed drawing of the comic book superhero, Batman, with the words "Happy Birthday Johnathan" written in bold letters. Drawing different superheroes was one of the things that his father did quite often during his time in jail, and often presented them to little John during the weekend visits. According to a feature story written by Eric Prisbell of the *Washington Post*, it is still cherished by the family to this day.

In 1998, Wall's father was diagnosed with liver cancer and was released from prison a month early as his condition became worse over time. Because of his father's deteriorating health over the next year, Wall's mother and father decided to take Wall and his two sisters on a beach vacation in August 1999. The family played on the beach, went out to eat, and enjoyed each other. It was at this time that Wall Sr. told his son to always try to be a better man and to be the first member of his family to go to college.

On the final day of the vacation, Wall's father had a hemorrhage and collapsed on the hotel floor. He died the next day in the hospital. In the earlier mentioned *Washington Post* article, Wall described how he remembers, in vivid detail, walking into the hotel bathroom where the tub was filled with blood. He could smell hemorrhaging and heard the sound of his mother crying and an ambulance siren growing louder as it approached the hotel the family was staying. His father passed away at the age of 52.

Although John's dad had given him sound advice in his final days, Wall suffered from the lack of a fatherly figure in his youth. This created a lot of anger inside Wall, which is a common issue among young boys who lose their father to prison, divorce, or death. Many of his episodes were during his grade school years and through middle school. This made it hard for everyone to approach him – his family, teachers, coaches, and classmates. He admitted that he even gave trouble to his babysitter, who was his stepsister from his mom's previous relationship. The effect of his father's death led to John rejecting any adult authority figure, especially male ones.

"Just so much anger built up," Wall said in an interview with the Washington Post in June 2010. "I was mad at everything. I did not trust coaches and people. Anytime somebody told me something, I just said, 'You don't know what you're talking about.' I did not want to believe nobody for some reason." Though such an outlook on life was a negative part of John's growth early on, it was an acceptable component of a young man's development.

His mother and elder sister worked their hardest to put food on the table, and John recalled how his mom would get off from her work as a maid at a local hotel to pick him up from school, tend to him for a few hours, and then take off for a different job. She would then return in the morning to rest, make Wall breakfast, and then start working again. At first, Wall did not follow his mother's path of hard work and developed a lack of respect for authority. He repeatedly got into fights and talked back to his teachers in elementary and middle school.

There were times when it got so bad that his mother would wait in the parking lot outside of the school because she knew the odds were in favor of him being sent home within the first two hours of the day. She did that because the family lived about 30 minutes away, so it was more of a convenience for her to just wait than to head back home after dropping him off at school. There were a lot of fights that took place during his childhood. One of these fights includes a time when 10-year-old Wall swung an aluminum bat at a much larger 14-year-old boy who took Wall's turn to bat. This led to a very long fight where they punched each other senseless with small two-minute breaks thrown in.

Other than the fights, another remarkable thing about John's childhood was that he spent lots of time on the basketball court where he lit up the local parks and gyms. However, his attitude was just as bad on the court. A youth basketball coach named LeVelle Moton, who is now the head coach at North Carolina Central University, let the impoverished Wall, who was 11 years old at the time, attend his basketball camp for free. The problem with Wall was that when things went against what he was hoping for, he would react negatively and violently like a time bomb that was ticking closer to an explosion. In the *Washington Post*, Moton explained that he attempted to change his behavior multiple times. However, after Wall repeatedly ignored Moton's lessons and argued with the referees, Moton was forced to kick him out.

At this point, there were a lot of worries about whether Wall would acknowledge his anger problem and find a way to control his emotions. At the time, signs showed that he was not heading in the right direction in his life, and something needed to be done immediately. One thing that was evident about John was that he had a passion for playing well on the basketball court because he felt that it would make his father, who was watching from heaven, proud of his accomplishments. One year after being kicked out of the program,

Wall returned with a different mindset and showed a more positive attitude.

Things began to improve for Wall when he met Brian and Dwon Clifton, who coached an Amateur Athletic Union (AAU) team called D-One. Unlike many AAU recruiters who latched onto young prospects like a parasite in the hopes for a cut from an eventual NBA paycheck, the Cliftons, first and foremost, looked out for Wall. John joined D-One and the Cliftons instantly made him the star of the team. However, that did not mean that Wall would be allowed to do as he pleased.

The Cliftons ordered Wall to shave off the braids he wore as a symbol of defiance and tried their best to teach him maturity. Wall's mother, likewise, did what she could. In middle school, John Wall was a better football player than basketball player, taking advantage of his blinding speed and athleticism to play running back, wide receiver, and safety. Frances, however, forbade Wall from playing football because she thought that the sport was too dangerous. She also warned the young Wall that if he never changed his attitude and shaped up, he would never develop into a great player.

Two years after being cut from Moton's youth basketball program, Wall would find himself playing in an AAU camp that Moton was officiating. He admitted that he intentionally made a few bad calls against Wall to see if his attitude had changed. What he found was a different Wall who would put the ball down and get into his defensive position without any shouting, yelling, or any form of visible or verbal anger towards Moton. Because of that change in combination with his performance on the court, Moton would later announce that Wall was the camp's Most Valuable Player. It was a way for Moton to celebrate how well he had matured because he feared that John's anger issues would eventually lead him to being killed by someone who did not like his attitude.

Chapter 2: High School Years

Despite the advice from those who cared for him, Wall continued to struggle with authority. In high school, Wall first played for Garner Magnet High School in Garner, North Carolina, and had two active years as part of the varsity team. During his sophomore year in the 2005-2006 season, Wall helped the Trojans to a 16-5 record overall, but they were unable to advance to the state playoffs at the 4A level.

Before his junior year began, the family moved to Raleigh and Wall joined Broughton High School. Cocky and full of himself, Wall assumed that he would be part of the varsity team, especially considering that the team was just average with a record of 9-9 the season before Wall moved to North Carolina. However, instead of becoming a star player with the Capitals in purple and gold, he was cut from the team due to the attitude that still lingered from his past. After talking to his mother and the Cliftons about what do to next, Wall transferred to Word of God Christian Academy in Raleigh,

North Carolina, where Brian Clifton was the head coach at the time. John Wall was still with a very successful program.

Word of God helped to improve Wall's temper and intellect. Wall was required to maintain a 2.4 grade point average to stay on the varsity team, and Word of God Coach Levi Beckwith worked on improving his attitude. In one game, the Word of God Holy Rams gave up a 20-point lead with Wall sitting on the bench. Coach Beckwith sent Wall back into the game when the Rams led by just two points. As he prepared to check in, Wall muttered that he should not even bother to play. Beckwith overheard what he said and ordered him back to the bench. While Word of God lost, the experience taught Wall that Beckwith was not going to let him say or do as he pleased, even if it meant that Word of God might lose games. If he wanted to play, he would have to behave. That would mean not saying demeaning things to his teammates when they missed layups and working on facial expressions that were just as damaging as saying something negative.

Under the tutelage of Beckwith and the continued support of his mother, Wall's attitude finally began to improve. He repeated his junior year to ensure that he had four years of high school basketball under his belt. During the 2007-2008 season, the team finished 31-3 and defeated United Faith Christian Academy in the 1A state championship – a season where Wall was not a factor due to his problems. But the team had some success, and John attracted attention from colleges across the country.

He averaged 22.1 points, nine assists, and eight rebounds in his final year of high school basketball with Word of God Christian Academy. After finishing with a regular-season record of 14-8, Word of God made it all the way to North Carolina's 1A state championship. The team lost their first game in the SEIC Tournament to Trinity Christian, 75-66, on February 21, 2009. But after that, the team was able to bounce back with a 90-36 win over Ridgecroft High School on February 24, 2009. Next was a 71-48 win over Wayne Country Day High School on February 26, 2009, and a 63-51 revenge win over Trinity Christian on February 27, 2009, in the 1A state semi-final game.

The momentum took them to the state championship game where they lost in the finals against United Faith Christian Academy, 56-53, because of a miraculous 40-foot buzzer-beater from United Faith's Ian Miller. Wall scored 11 points in that game. The John Wall of the past used to demean his teammates who failed to make easy shots, but now he had become a capable passer and never insulted or trashed anyone, even his opponents.

Outside of high-school basketball, Wall continued to play for the Clifton brothers and D-One in AAU basketball and built a national profile. He entered several national tournaments across the country such as the 2007 Reebok All-American Camp and 2009 Jordan Brand Classic. Wall scored 28 points at the Reebok All-American camp against future NBA lottery pick Brandon Jennings. In August 2008, Wall would become one of the highlight players in the Elite 24 Hoops

Classic held in Brooklyn, New York. He would score 10 points in an effort that helped him earn a share of the MVP honors with other top basketball prospects such as Lance Stephenson, Maalik Wayns, and Dominic Cheek. He would later score 13 points and 11 assists in the 2009 Nike Hoops Summit. Such impressive performances showcased Wall as one of the top prospects in the nation. Standing at six-foot-four with terrific athleticism and great court vision, everyone knew that he would have a bright future in the NBA after he left college.

In 2009, Rivals.com put Wall at the top of their 150 top prospect rankings as a five-star recruit. He found himself listed above other future NBA players like DeMarcus Cousins, Avery Bradley, and Lance Stephenson. In a 2008 scouting report, Wall was described by expert Jerry Meyer as being very fast. Furthermore, he described John Wall as someone who plays basketball with plenty of ball-handling skills and savviness on the court, which made him look like a veteran. John was also praised for his ability to get the ball to his teammates while finishing offensive rushes to the basket for layups and small jump-shots, even though he was not considered the best at jumping.

However, a ringing question at that time was where John Wall would go to college, or if he was going to college at all. In 2005, the NBA and its players ratified a new collective bargaining agreement that set the minimum age for NBA players to 19 and a year removed from high school. The agreement was designed to prevent high school players from directly joining the NBA. However, Wall's circumstances were unusual since he was a fifth-year senior. Whether he could have ascended to the NBA was hard to say, but before a decision could be reached, Wall declared that he would enter college. Thus, as Wall's senior year began, he remained unsure of where he would go.

In addition to the struggles of deciding which college to go to in his senior year, Wall suffered from other problems. In 2009, Wall and two friends were charged with breaking into an abandoned home. There was no sign of forced entry, and the three men took nothing, so the charges were dropped. However, many college coaches were concerned due to his past maturity issues. On top of that, an eligibility issue appeared during his senior year. Wall's coach, Brian Clifton, was once a sports agent for FIBA. While he no longer worked as an agent, he was technically registered as one, which meant that any standard sports expenses such as food and clothing that Clifton gave Wall were illegal under NCAA rules. Wall had to pay $800 back to Clifton, which the estimated cost of the items, and was suspended for his first game in the NCAA. But neither of those problems compared to the third issue. Wall's mother, who had worked so hard over the years, developed a brain aneurysm in his senior year.

With a lot of health issues in the family, Wall was adjusting his college search to keep his mother in mind. The state of North Carolina has many great basketball schools, most notably the University of North Carolina and Duke University. Wall seriously considered going to one of them to stay close to his mother. There was also an offer made by North Carolina State, but their program did not have established head coaches such as Mike Krzyzewski (Duke) and Roy Williams (UNC).

Fortunately, Frances recovered, and Wall could take his pick among schools across the country. This expanded his options to other nearby states like Texas, Tennessee, Florida, Kansas, and Kentucky. Wall visited Kansas as they held their ring ceremony for winning the 2008 NCAA National Championship tournament, and Baylor hired Dwon Clifton as an assistant, presumably to entice Wall. But rather than going to a school with a winning pedigree or someplace with familiar faces, Wall had the wisdom to look for a school that could develop him into a legitimate NBA star.

Wall looked long and hard at Memphis, especially their coach, John Calipari. Calipari ran a "dribble drive" offense that gave the ball to athletic point guards, and he had achieved great success using it with future NBA players such as Derrick Rose and Tyreke Evans. Wall felt that he could follow in their legacy, and he was pleased with the fact that Calipari was honest. He told Wall up front that he would have to work incredibly hard if he wanted to follow in the footsteps of Rose and Evans. Rose was selected as the first overall pick to the Chicago Bulls in the 2008 NBA Draft, and Evans was chosen as the fourth pick to the Sacramento Kings a year later. Confident that Calipari's system would give him a chance to develop into a star point guard and a future high lottery pick, Wall finally decided to join Calipari.

Calipari was hired by the University of Kentucky shortly after the 2009 NCAA National Championship tournament ended in a 102-91 loss to Missouri in the Sweet 16 round. It made sense for Calipari considering the success he had with the Tigers: nine seasons with a total of 252 wins and multiple visits to the NCAA National Championship tournament. However, 38 of those wins from the 2008 team were forfeited due to NCAA violations.

Because of the rapport that he had built with Coach Calipari, Wall decided to join Calipari in Kentucky. The commitment was made official on May 19, 2009.

Chapter 3: College Years at the University of Kentucky

When John Wall arrived in Kentucky, he was a celebrity because he was a student-athlete. The Kentucky Wildcats had underachieved for the previous several years after Tubby Smith and Billy Gillispie struggled to get the team beyond the second round of the NCAA National Championship tournament. Kentucky was often in the middle of the pack of the Southeastern Conference (SEC) and had no more than 22 total wins.

Both the fans and the team hoped to return to elite college basketball with the arrival of Wall, Calipari, and fellow upcoming freshmen Demarcus Cousins, Eric Bledsoe, and Daniel Orton. Wall's preseason introduction to the Kentucky students was not on a basketball court, but rather on a stage with music blaring, lights flashing, and crowds cheering as if they were at a rock concert. As the Kentucky announcer shouted his name, Wall stood above the stage wearing earbuds and blue Kentucky warm-ups. He danced with the crowd with a wide grin on his face.

Moments like those were the upside of being the best-known person on the Kentucky campus, but being a celebrity comes with its downsides as well. Whenever John Wall walked to campus for class, he pulled a hood over his head and headphones over his ears. He did this to avoid being accosted by the relentless hordes of autograph-seekers that swarmed him. While Wall could have just rebuffed them all, he did not want to appear rude. The desire to not hurt anyone's feelings is a sharp contrast from the immature high school player who would not hesitate to trash his teammates. College is often considered a chance for young adults to build a new identity and be able to make a real change from what their past had to show. Therefore, those familiar with Wall were seeing a much different Wall they knew during his childhood in North Carolina.

Wall was forced to sit out the first exhibition game of Kentucky's season as punishment for the eligibility problem. But on November 6, 2009, he made his exhibition debut for Kentucky. Playing against Clarion University of Pennsylvania, Wall had 27 points and nine assists in less than 30 minutes in a 117-52 blowout. At the beginning of the 2009-2010 season, Wall was not eligible to play in the team's 75-59 win over Morehead State University on November 13, 2009. It

20

was a game where some of the other star players stepped up, including Bledsoe's 24 points, and Patrick Patterson, who collected 20 points and 12 rebounds.

Wall's first regular season game was against the Miami (Ohio) Redhawks, a small mid-major program out of the Mid-American Conference. The Redhawks' guard, Kenny Hayes, hit a deep three-pointer to tie the game at 70 with six seconds left. Calipari wondered whether he should call timeout, but before he could decide, Wall raced down the court and sank the game-winner, giving the team a 72-70 victory. The game-winner helped highlight an incredible debut for the young freshman with 19 points to lead the Wildcats. It was all thanks to making four out of his nine field goals and 10 out of 14 free throws. Two of his teammates also had double-doubles. Patterson had 17 points and ten rebounds while Cousins had 10 points and ten rebounds.

It was not the last great performance by Wall that season. In his next game, Wall had 21 points after shooting seven out of 13 field goals in support of Cousins' 27 points and 18 rebounds in a 102-92 victory over Sam Houston State on November 19, 2009. Wall would later get his first ever double-double in the Wildcats' 92-63 win on November 21, 2009. Wall led Kentucky with 21 points and 11 assists while making eight out of his 12 field goal attempts and five out of six free throws. This would be one of the times that he had more than ten assists in a game, which was one of the strongest qualities of his game when he was a senior at Word of God Christian Academy back in

Raleigh, North Carolina. On November 30, 2009, Wall made 14 assists and 12 points in Kentucky's 94-57 win over UNC-Asheville. About a month later, Wall would have a season-high of 16 assists for a school record in the Wildcats' 104-61 win over Hartford on December 29, 2009. What was equally impressive about this performance was that Wall only had one turnover in his 30 minutes on the court.

While showing his skills in passing and shooting, he would also demonstrate that he was able to make big plays when he needed to. One of the best examples was on December 9, 2009, at the University of Connecticut during a non-conference game held at Madison Square Garden in New York City, which has hosted some of the best athletes throughout the history of the National Basketball Association. It was during this game with the UConn Huskies that Wall would lead the team with 25 points after making 10 out of 16 field goals, highlighted by a game-clinching basket with 30 seconds left to give Kentucky the 64-61 victory. Wall also had six steals on defense in one of his best all-around performances on both sides of the court.

While Wall put up huge games one after another, Kentucky looked unstoppable with their influx of freshmen talent. They won their first 19 games in one of the school's best starts in 44 years before losing to South Carolina on January 26, 2010, 68-62. Wall had 19 points in that game despite making only 37.5 percent of his field goals (6 out of 16). He would have a few more bad shooting games, but Wall was very efficient throughout most of the season. While he was mostly known for scoring and providing assists to his fellow Wildcats, Wall had ten rebounds to go along with his 22 points in Kentucky's 66-55 win over Alabama on February 9, 2010. One week later on February 16, 2010, Wall had another ten rebounds along with eight assists and 18 points in an 81-75 victory at Mississippi State University in one of his most extensive games with a total of 44 minutes.

Wall would also find himself becoming a stronger player as they continued to climb the standings in the SEC. This included his best shooting performance on March 3, 2010, where he was 8 out of 10 from the field, including three out of five from beyond the three-point line, for a total of 24 points in Kentucky's 80-68 win. By the end of the regular season, the Kentucky Wildcats would finish with a 29-2 record and would be 14-2 against the rest of the SEC to give them the top seed in the conference tournament.

That dominance against the remainder of the SEC would continue in the SEC Tournament as the Wildcats defeated Alabama, 73-67, on March 12, 2010. It was a game where Wall had 23 points after making 7 out of 12 field goals and 9 out of 13 free throws in addition to collecting seven rebounds and five assists. In the SEC semifinal game, Wall only had 14 points but had nine assists and six rebounds in the team's 74-45 blowout victory over the Tennessee Volunteers on March 13, 2010. But Wall would have one of his best games in the SEC Conference Tournament Championship on March 14, 2010.

The Wildcats were down 64-62 in the final seconds of regulation when Eric Bledsoe intentionally missed a free throw to get Kentucky the ball back. Wall grabbed the ball and missed the potential game-winner, but his teammate, Cousins, was there to tip the ball in and force the game into overtime. In overtime, Wall scored seven of Kentucky's 11 points, and the Wildcats prevailed 75-74. It was Kentucky's first SEC tournament win since 2004. Coach Calipari implored that fans not to cut down the basketball nets to celebrate the victory, saying that they could do it when Kentucky won the NCAA tournament.

At first, Calipari's promise of an NCAA tournament seemed to ring true. The Wildcats were the second-ranked team in the polls and were given the top seed in the East Regional section of the overall 65-team bracket. The Wildcats destroyed East Tennessee State in their first round game, 100-71, on March 18, 2010, where Wall would score 17 points and 11 assists to his teammates in only 29 minutes in the blowout victory. Wall was one of the top players despite the high scores coming from Bledsoe (29 points) and Patterson (22 points). Large margins were a common trend for Wall and the Wildcats. They continued to be the favorites to possibly win the NCAA National Championship, especially since the Kansas Jayhawks, who were considered the top overall seed in the tournament, lost in the second round. The loss was in an upset to the ninth-seeded Northern Iowa Panthers, 69-67, on March 20, 2010, in St. Louis, Missouri.

Wall would make another significant contribution on March 20, 2010, in their second-round victory over the Wake Forest Demon Deacons, 90-60. He only scored 14 points on five out of seven field goals, including three out of four from behind the three-point arc and four out of six free throws in just 29 minutes. Once again, Cousins was one of the key scorers with 19 points in that game, but it was Darius Miller who led the team with 20 points to help the Wildcats reach the Sweet 16 round – something that Kentucky had not been able to do for several years.

But when you are a top-ranked team at that stage, upsets can happen, and the Wildcats wanted to be prepared for the Cornell Big Red out of the Ivy League. Kentucky kept their pace defensively and were able to advance over Cornell with a 62-45 win on March 25, 2010. Wall may not have had a lot of points with only eight after shooting four out of nine from the field, but he was able to collect seven rebounds and eight assists which helped his Kentucky teammates. Cousins had 16 points and Bledsoe's 12 points.

After their first three games, the Wildcats were winning their contests by an average of over 25 points per game to help them get to the Elite Eight round. Furthermore, with Kansas having lost earlier and other teams falling sooner than expected, Kentucky was left as the favorite team to win in the NCAA tournament. There was a lot of talk going around that Coach Calipari was developing yet another powerhouse college basketball team after years of success with the Memphis Tigers. The road seemed wide open, but in NCAA ball, fortunes can rise and fade with just one game, especially when it is just one round away from the illustrious Final Four.

On March 27, 2010, the Wildcats faced off in the East Regional Finals against the West Virginia Mountaineers. West Virginia collapsed the paint and doubled and even triple-teamed Cousins, forcing Kentucky and Wall to hit jump shots. Kentucky struggled to hit shots even at the free throw line where they went 16 for 29. By contrast, West Virginia hit 43% of their three-point shots, and their swarming defense harassed the inexperienced Kentucky team. Kentucky would lose 73-66. Wall had 19 points, nine rebounds, and five assists. However, this was overshadowed by five turnovers as well as 7 for 18 shooting for the game with only one basket out of five attempts from beyond the three-point line for a total of 38.9% made shots from the field.

Kentucky's finish to the season may have been sooner than they hoped, but it did not take away Wall's impressive season. He averaged 16.6 points, 6.5 assists, and 4.3 rebounds for the season on 46% shooting from the field to help the Kentucky Wildcats finish the season with a 35-3 overall record. He was named the SEC Player of the Year and made the First-Team All-American. Likewise, he also received the SEC Tournament Most Valuable Player award. Wall had already been viewed as the number one pick in the 2010 NBA Draft when he entered Kentucky and he had done absolutely nothing to dissuade draft experts. Scouts raved about his quickness and explosiveness, excellent passing ability, sound defensive instincts, and above all, his competitive drive and maturity.

When scouts talked about maturity, they referred to Wall's temperament on the court. But Wall was more than just a basketball player in Kentucky. In the summer, before he formally joined Kentucky, Wall took summer courses in Lexington. He sat at the front of the class and earned a perfect 4.0 grade point average for the season. He spoke to ESPN about how he earned a 3.5 GPA in his second semester, and that his favorite subject was Math. This was becoming a much different Wall than the one his family and coaches know in high school. He was turning things around for the better in his life, and it was leading to a chance to be a star in the NBA because he would leave Kentucky after playing only one season – something that Calipari was used to in Memphis with stars like Derrick Rose.

Chapter 4: John's NBA Career

Getting Drafted

There are few franchises with a history as disappointing as the Washington Wizards. Since losing in the NBA Finals back in 1979, the Wizards have never won more than 45 games in a season, the longest streak in the NBA. A core of Gilbert Arenas, Caron Butler, and Antawn Jamison showed promise in the mid-2000s, but it was derailed by injuries and three straight playoff defeats to LeBron James and the Cleveland Cavaliers. That team finally saw its end after trades moved Butler and Jamison while injuries slowed Arenas down.

While Wall was leading the Kentucky Wildcats to victory after victory over the 2009-2010 basketball season, the Wizards were derailed by a gun scandal. Arenas and teammate Javaris Crittenton had pointed loaded guns at each other and Arenas had stored loaded guns in the Wizards' locker room. When Arenas appeared recalcitrant in a pre-game stunt where he pretended to shoot his teammates with finger guns, the NBA suspended Arenas indefinitely. One of the lowest points in the season was a 16-game losing streak that included a 102-74 loss to the Milwaukee Bucks on March 5, 2010.

Right when things looked darkest for Washington, they had the great fortune of winning the 2010 NBA Draft Lottery and the number one pick. They earned the seed after having some of the best odds in the NBA Draft's lottery because of a 26-56 record to finish in the cellar of the Eastern Conference's Southeast Division. The Wizards were 26th out of the NBA's 30 teams, averaging only 96.2 points per game while giving up an average of about 101 points per game with many poor performances in front of their annoyed fans at the Verizon Center in DC.

Luckily for the Wizards, they could easily fast track their rebuilding process by selecting the most talented player in the class with their number one pick. Based on what was seen from that draft class, no other player came close to the talents, skills, and abilities of John Wall, who would stake his claim as the consensus top draft pick.

Other players could have been good enough to challenge John Wall for that top spot. His Kentucky teammate DeMarcus Cousins was as promising a center as one can be because of his combination of size, strength, and skill at that position. However, the apparent problem with Cousins was his temper and demeanor. He was widely regarded as uncoachable because of his hot-headedness and his refusal to listen to the coaching staff.

While two other players in that draft class would eventually become All-Stars, both Gordon Hayward and Paul George did not have the combination of skill, athleticism, and college basketball success that John Wall enjoyed in Kentucky. Wall was a ready product compared to the other prospects that had potential. Thus, he was widely unchallenged as the potential top pick.

At 6'4", John Wall had more than enough size for a point guard. In fact, with a wingspan nearing 6'10", he was already taller and longer than most other playmakers in the league.[i] While Wall was a physical specimen at the point guard position because of his height and length, the former Kentucky star point guard was most impressive in the athleticism department.

John Wall was athleticism personified. With the ball in his hands, Wall was so blazingly fast that most of his memorable moments in college involved plays wherein he would get the ball from his rebounder in the backcourt and would be seen making highlight dunks or layups at the other end of the hardwood floor two seconds later. In a league that had seen its share of spitfire guards like Allen Iverson, Derrick Rose, and Russell Westbrook, John Wall was still impressively fast. Add the fact that he could also jump high at his position with his 40-inch vertical leap.

Because of John Wall's physical gifts and athletic abilities, he was often compared to the likes of Derrick Rose and Russell Westbrook who, at that time, were using their athleticism to dominate opposing point guards and ushering in a new era of backcourt playmakers. However, Wall was a bigger and arguably better athlete than both Rose and Westbrook. From a physical standpoint alone, there was almost no doubting that John Wall had the makings of a future All-Star like Rose or Westbrook.[ii]

Some would even argue that, from a physical standpoint alone, John Wall was a better athlete than either Rose or Westbrook. He was a lot taller and longer than those two athletic point guards. Rose was barely 6'2" without shoes on and his 6'3" draft measurement was already generous. Meanwhile, Westbrook was a little bit taller than Derrick Rose, and his arms were just as long. John Wall was both taller and longer than Rose and Westbrook. On top of that, his max vertical leap was just the same as Rose's despite the fact that he was taller while he would also tally a faster sprinting time than Russell Westbrook did during the NBA combine. Judging from those physical and athletic

30

gifts alone, one would already see that Wall was going down the path that those other two NBA All-Stars had walked.

While John Wall was already a cut above the rest of his draft class just from his size and athleticism, his overall skill level made him the potential superstar prospect he was believed to be. There was almost nothing he could not do on the floor, whether it was on offense, defense, or in any other aspects of the game of basketball.

Offensively, Wall relied primarily on his blazing speed to execute transition plays or blow by his defenders at the half-court setting. But his athleticism was not the bulk of his offense. John Wall had a good understanding of how to break defenses down. Wall gets to the basket to showcase his array of finishing abilities by making minced meat out of the defense.

When attacking the basket, John Wall could finish high, especially with his combination of size and length. And whenever it would get too difficult to finish plainly above the outstretched arms of defenders, the athletic point guard would contort his body in midair, much like Dwyane Wade. He could even twist his body up in the air to make impossible layups that only a player with his combination of size, athleticism, and skill could do.

However, Wall was not a reckless attacker on the offensive end, unlike some of the younger athletic point guards that came before him. He did not always go at full speed unless he needed to. Defenders would often get off-balanced because of how great Wall always was on switching to the maximum gear from his slowest pace. He had an incredibly quick acceleration that he knew how to utilize to catch sleeping defenders off-guard.

Though Wall was picky about when he wanted to use his full speed, he still looked like a player in control whenever he ran at his fastest pace. When you saw John Wall running like a gazelle on the offense, one would think that he was attacking recklessly. However, he always seemed like he had a plan of attack because he also had the rare ability to switch paces at full speed. This allowed him to pick apart opposing defenses for easy scoring opportunities for himself or his teammates.

Despite how good of a prospect as John Wall was regarding the scoring he could potentially bring to any NBA team, the most intriguing skill he had was his passing. In college, John Wall was never at the top of the nation concerning dishing out assists. Nevertheless, that part of his game was underrated since his playmaking efficiency was one of the best in the country. John Wall had a high assist per field goal ratio, which meant that the assists he was dishing out compared to the shots he was taking proved how unselfish of a point guard he truly was.[iii]

John Wall's ability to break down defenses using his speed and athleticism made him one of the best drive and dish players in college. However, he showed that he was not a one-trick pony in the assist department. He has also displayed a lot of creativity in making plays for his teammates outside of his ability to drive and dish.

On the offensive side of things, John Wall was the perfect point guard that could usher in a bright future for any time and one that fits the model of a playmaker of the incoming, new era of the NBA. He had the size, athleticism, scoring abilities, and playmaking skills that made him a player that could score the ball himself or create shots for other players.

Offensively, John Wall was a gem that could instantly make a difference for a team that lacked production in that department. Other than his production on that end of the floor, Wall was also a productive defensive player. With his size alone, he could defend both guard positions well. His length allowed him to smother his opponents to the point of frustrating their ability to score the ball.

With his athleticism, John Wall has also proven to be a ball hawk on defense. He could smother and frustrate his own man while also showing the ability to play passing lanes and get a lot of steals. And, for a guard, Wall has also used his size and length perfectly to block shots at the rim.[iii] Judging from the statistics he posted on the defensive end when he was in Kentucky, it was clear that John Wall understood how to use his physical gifts on the defensive side of the floor.

However, despite all the positives that John Wall could bring to an NBA team on both ends of the court, there were also weaknesses that they had to gamble with. Offensively, Wall did not have a lot of weaknesses. But the few he had were certainly causes for concerns for the Washington Wizards, who needed a perfect offensive player to put their rebuilding process on the fast track.

The most glaring of John Wall's offensive weaknesses was his inability to score at the half court. Using his speed and athleticism, John Wall came into the draft arguably faster than any point guard in recent memory. He puts that speed to good use in the open court and fast break opportunities by quickly converting his shots on the other end or by setting up streaking teammates. However, he has never shown to be a similarly productive player during half-court sets.[iii]

In the half court, John Wall's field goal shooting drops from a whopping 77% in transition to 40% during set plays. His foul-drawing abilities also saw a decrease whenever he was forced to play a slow tempo style of basketball. Moreover, though Wall's ability to set up teammates in transition is well-documented, his playmaking skills also decline during set plays, especially the pick-and-roll, which is the most basic half-court play that point guards should excel at.[iii]

The biggest reason as to why John Wall's effectivity falls during half-court sets is his lack of a reliable jump shot. Similar to Derrick Rose and Russell Westbrook, Wall had to rely mainly on his athleticism on the offensive side of things since his jump shot needs a lot of refining, though his mechanics did not seem broken. Because of that, defenses often sagged on him during set plays to prevent him from slashing to the basket.[iii] They would rather gamble on Wall's jump shot than his ability to finish and score at the rim.

John Wall's perimeter shooting needed a lot of refining before it became a deadly weapon. He had not proven to be an effective player when left wide open. Wall was never seen to be very comfortable shooting jump shots with his feet set and with defenders still far away from defending his shot. He was often more comfortable with taking perimeter shots off the dribble, which also gave defenders time to close in on him compared to catch-and-shoot situations.

His in-between game also needed a lot of work. In the NBA, point guards utilize floaters and close-range jumpers more often because modern defenses have chosen to shut down the paint and three-point shot by yielding to the perimeter game more often. Given the amount of height point guards give up compared to paint defenders, they usually take a significant amount of perimeter shots or floating jumpers in the lane. However, John Wall, who relies on his athleticism and finishing ability to score in the paint, has not shown to favor in-between scoring moves that even an athletic point guard like Derrick Rose, who scores a lot using floaters, has been utilizing in the NBA.[iv]

Wall's basketball IQ and decision-making skills also drop significantly at the half court. With defenses sagging on him whenever he has the ball out on the perimeter, John Wall's offensive choices dwindle down to either shooting his inefficient jump shot or making plays for his teammates. However, because he is unable to break defenses down effectively at the half-court, Wall was often prone to turning the ball over due to bad decisions and ill-advised passes.[iii]

As a point guard that handles the ball a lot on offense, John Wall needed to work on his dribbling ability. Despite having the dribbling skills needed of a point guard in the NBA, Wall's ball handling did not seem to be on par with the speed he often played with. Compared to other point guards that could tear defenses down with their dribbling skills, Wall almost always favored using his speed and explosive first step in doing so.[iii] But when his superior athletic abilities got neutralized, John Wall became less useful in such situations.

But what was considered as John Wall's biggest weakness was that he was yet to develop a killer instinct and an aggressive mindset to take over games when he was needed to. What set Derrick Rose and Russell Westbrook apart from him was their relentless pursuit of aggressively attacking the basket in the hopes of drawing a foul or getting the basket through an athletic play. They also knew how to take over games. John Wall was not there yet. He was not as aggressive in trying to draw fouls, and his point guard mentality would rather have him make plays for teammates rather than take over the plays by himself. All the great ones know when to take over and when to have their killer instinct take hold of them. John Wall needed to develop that kind of a mindset.

Though John Wall had glaring weaknesses that could potentially prevent him from becoming a true superstar in the NBA, his supreme talent and intangibles were qualities that nobody could pass up. John Wall did not come in as a good offensive player alone but also brought a certain confident attitude that made him a famous player.

With his swagger and demeanor on the court, Wall could rally the crowd behind him and his team whenever they needed extra motivation. And whenever it got too competitive, he has also bailed Kentucky out in numerous clutch situations. Those intangibles were rare qualities to find in a player as young as John Wall coming into the NBA. There was arguably no reason to doubt his place as the top prospect in the class of 2010. The Wizards needed him.

At first, some analysts wondered whether the Wizards might select a different player in the draft. Since Arenas and Wall were both point guards who sought to score first, there was some concern about how they would fit together on the floor together. Without a doubt, Wall was still one of the most talented players in the NBA Draft. And it is hard not to select a player who is repeatedly rated as the top overall college prospect by NBA writers and experts. Only his fellow teammate, Demarcus Cousins, was comparable, and draft experts felt that Cousins had major attitude issues compared to Wall's temper problems back when he was in high school.

Understanding the importance of selecting talent over fit, the Washington Wizards selected Wall with the first pick. He was the first Kentucky Wildcat to be drafted with the top overall pick. It was an elementary choice, to be honest. He was the consensus pick no matter who had the top choice in the NBA Draft. John Wall was a generational talent that could instantly turn the hopes of a struggling franchise around. It was the simplest decision that the Wizards had to make during that offseason.

After the failures of the Arenas-Butler-Jamison years, the Wizards were looking to rebuild completely. While they were excited to grab Wall and would not have minded in the slightest if he led the Wizards to the playoffs as a rookie, the reality was that Wizards fans expected to be in the lottery for some time. Despite Wall's talents, the team roster was still facing tough times, especially since they had a combination of hard-headed young talents coupled with veterans who hampered the team's ability to rebuild because of their enormous contracts. But in any case, John Wall was part of what could be a long-term plan for the Washington Wizards, who finally found the player that could quickly usher in a new era for the franchise.

Rookie Season

Despite having enough talent and ability to make an immediate impact in the NBA, John Wall's rookie season was not going to be an easy one. The Washington Wizards were still undergoing a transformation and transition stage. Aside from having veterans that hampered their ability to sign young players, those veterans themselves were not perfect examples of what it was to be professional to young and talented, yet problematic, players such as Nick Young, Andray Blatche, and JaVale McGee. At only 19 years old, Wall was a young player that needed veteran guidance. Unfortunately, he had minimal of that in his rookie year.

In his NBA debut, Wall struggled to adjust quickly on October 28, 2010, as he faced off against the Orlando Magic, who had just made the Eastern Conference Finals in the last playoffs. Wall struggled to get his shots off against the defending Defensive Player of the Year Dwight Howard and finished with just 14 points after making only six out of 19 shots in the 112-83 loss at the Amway Center in Orlando, Florida.

But against lesser teams in the next two games with Atlanta and Philadelphia, Wall started to show his potential. After scoring 28 points and nine assists in a 99-95 loss to the Atlanta Hawks on October 30 at the Philips Arena in Atlanta, Georgia, Wall made his home debut against the Philadelphia 76ers on November 2, 2010. In front of a roaring Washington, DC, crowd, Wall danced the Dougie as the stadium announced his name. While he did have eight turnovers, he also had 29 points after making nine out of his 16 field goals (56.3 percent) and 11 out of 14 free throws. Wall also collected 13 assists and nine steals as the Wizards grabbed their first win of the season, 116-115, in overtime.

On November 10, 2010, Wall earned his first career triple-double in the NBA against the Houston Rockets with 19 points, 13 assists, and ten rebounds in a 98-91 win. It was quite the accomplishment for someone who was just in his sixth career game in the league. He was the third youngest NBA player ever to record a triple-double behind LeBron James and Lamar Odom, which is some great company to be a part of if you are a young star in the NBA.

Wanting to keep playing even while the Wizards were losing games, he rushed back after missing four games with a sprained left foot early in the season. This proved to be a mistake. Wall quickly picked up a knee injury that sidelined him for eight games in late November and December. When he returned, he struggled to get back into game shape. Over his next 18 games, Wall's shaky jumper, weak legs, and the lack of help around him meant that he struggled to score, shooting just 38 percent over December and January.

Meanwhile, Gilbert Arenas, who played 21 games that season while sharing backcourt duties with John Wall, was traded for Orlando's Rashard Lewis in the middle of December. While the move was questionable given that Lewis was past his prime and that he had a contract worth about $20 million for the next two seasons, the move allowed Wall to own the playmaking role while providing the young star a shooter at the wings. This was because the Wizards had built a weak team with few shooters and more athletes than actual basketball players. Even though the team was poorly designed, Wall put up solid numbers night in and night out.

One of his worst individual performances came on December 26, 2010, on the road against the veteran-led San Antonio Spurs in a 94-80 loss at the AT&T Center in San Antonio, Texas. Wall finished the game with just under 20 minutes of time on the court with four points on just two made field goals out of nine attempts, along with six rebounds and four assists. Despite the high number of points scored in several of his games with the Wizards in his rookie season, Wall had nine games where his scoring output fell within single digits.

Even though Wall struggled to score, he still passed the ball well for assists, thus belying the idea that he was a shoot-first point guard. On January 5, 2011, he equaled his then-career high in assists with 14 in a loss to the 76ers. Twelve days later, he reached a new high of 15 dimes together with 19 respectable points in a win over the Utah Jazz and Deron Williams, who was playing some of his best basketball as a star point guard at that time.

In January, he averaged 10 and a half assists per game while incurring only a little less than four turnovers per game in the process, an excellent assist to turnover ratio. In that month alone, John Wall had nine games of assisting on at least ten baskets. While Wall was a good scorer at the point guard position, he was quickly becoming an even better playmaker despite not being known in that department when he was still applying for the NBA Draft. Consequently, from January to April 2011, Wall was nominated as the Eastern Conference Rookie of the Month.

As the All-Star Game rolled around, Wall was chosen to play in the NBA Rising Stars Game where the Rookies defeated the Sophomores of the league, 148-140, on February 18, 2011, at the Staples Center in Los Angeles, California. While his former Kentucky teammate, DeMarcus Cousins, led everyone with 33 points, Wall made his impact with a total of 22 assists against only five turnovers, which was good enough for Wall to be named 2011 Game MVP. As the seconds ticked away in the rookie game, Wall walked up to his All-Star coach, Boston Celtics legend Kevin McHale, and broke out into the Dougie once again to the roars of the crowd, a memory that started to make Wall develop more of a cult following among the dedicated NBA audience.

As Wall's legs began to grow more confident, he became more assertive in his scoring role. After averaging less than 14 points a game in both December and January, his scoring averages improved to 16 points in February. He started to reach the 20-point mark regularly after the All-Star break, which could be credited to the big performance in that Rising Stars game.

In the first game back from the break, Wall nearly had his second triple-double after scoring 15 points, ten assists, and eight rebounds in a 113-96 loss to the Indiana Pacers on February 22, 2011, at the Verizon Center in DC. A few days later, Wall would make 46.7% of his field goals (7 out of 15) in nearly 39 minutes in the Wizards' 121-113 loss while visiting the Miami Heat on February 25, 2011 – a game where he would also score 24 points and collect 12 assists. His numbers would continue to improve as the season continued despite Washington struggling to get out of the bottom of the division standings.

John Wall would only get better in March. While his abilities in scoring and assisting were already well-documented in only his rookie season in the league, Wall was quickly becoming a good rebounding point guard, much like his similarly athletic playmaking predecessors, Rose and Westbrook. In that month, he had five games of rebounding seven or more misses, and in two of those performances, he had double-digit rebounds.

On March 23, 2011, in a battle against fellow rookie Blake Griffin, Wall scored a new career high of 32 points in a double-overtime game where he played 51 minutes, another career high. The Clippers won, 127-119, thanks to a triple-double from Blake Griffin (33 points, 17 rebounds, and ten assists), but it was hailed as an excellent battle between the two great rookies. Wall also had ten assists and five rebounds in that game. He was also very consistent from the line in many of the games in his rookie season. That included 14 out of 16 from the foul line after making only 6 out of 15 total field goals to finish with 26 points, 12 assists, and six rebounds on April 5, 2011, in a 107-105 victory over the Detroit Pistons.

Despite Wall's already apparent abilities as a future star and franchise player that could practically do everything on the floor for his team, the Washington Wizards were still a confused and struggling team that was still finding its identity and the optimal combination of players on the court. Everything had to go through John Wall, who led his team in assists and was second in scoring barely behind Andray Blatche. The Wizards, despite the brilliance of their rookie, saw several streaks of losses cut off by one or two consecutive wins in what was another disappointing year.

Nevertheless, John Wall finished his rookie season averaging 16.4 points, 8.3 assists, and 4.6 rebounds per game. The team would finish in the last place in the Eastern Conference's Southeast Division with an overall record of 23-59. No one could blame Wall, who finished the season with 26 total double-doubles in just 64 total starts in his first season in the NBA. John Wall was also the top assist man among rookies and was seventh overall in the entire league. He was also in the top 20 concerning total steals for the season. Unfortunately for Wall, Blake Griffin had taken the NBA by storm.

The 2009 number-one draft pick had missed the entire 2009-2010 season with a patella injury, but in his debut season, he made ESPN headlines with thunderous dunk after dunk. Wall also made the All-Star team, the first rookie to be selected by coaches to the All-Star Game since the great Tim Duncan. The former Oklahoma Sooner had averaged 22.5 points per game, along with averages of 12.1 rebounds (8.8 on defense per game), 3.8 assists, and nearly one block per game. He finished all 82 games in the season with 63 double-doubles and two triple-doubles to help the Clippers finish with a slightly-improved

32-50 record and to get the team out of the basement of the Western Conference's Pacific Division.

While Wall's performance would have won him the Rookie of the Year in most years, he was completely overshadowed by Griffin, who was unanimously voted for the award. Wall still finished second place in voting by a huge margin and was nominated to the All-Rookie First Team. However, Blake Griffin's phenomenal rookie year was not the only reason why John Wall was not considered for the top prize for rookies. There were also still a lot of flaws in his game.

John Wall had an awful field goal percentage in his rookie year. He was a great attacker in open-court situations and an excellent finisher at the basket. However, what prevented him from shooting well from the floor were his struggles from the perimeter. From three feet from the basket all the way to the three-point line, he barely shot above 30% from the perimeter. The only time he shot well was when he was under or above the basket.

One other problem in his game during his rookie year in the NBA was that he was dreadfully turnover-prone. In a league full of ball-dominant point guards and playmakers, John Wall was second in the league in turnovers at 3.8. And though he was in the top 10 in assists that season, his turnovers canceled out the number of dimes he was dishing out. He had an assist-turnover ratio of 2.20, which ranked only 45th in the NBA.

Despite the glaring weaknesses he had shown in his rookie season, John Wall still had an excellent rookie season that could even be argued to be a better one than that of some of the other athletic point guards that came before him. He had shown the same attacking mentality that would soon be worthy of an All-Star while maintaining his primary role as a passer and playmaker, albeit a turnover-prone one, as he was still learning and adjusting his game to the NBA.

Sophomore Slump

In his sophomore year, Wall knew that he had to do a lot of work to become an NBA star despite getting a good start with the accolades he received after the 2010-2011 season. He hired a personal chef to change his diet and worked on his jump shot and physique in Lexington, Kentucky with his old coach, John Calipari, at the University of Kentucky where he helped the Wildcat team advance to the Elite Eight and won a total of 35 games.

Unfortunately, his hopes of playing for a better Washington Wizards team in his second season looked as if they were to be dashed by an NBA lockout, which lasted for the first month of the 2011-2012 season. This was caused by the expiration of a collective bargaining agreement (CBA) that was made in 2005. The lockout lasted about 161 days with tough negotiations between the players and team owners in regards to items like the division of the league's overall revenue and how the league structured things like the salary cap and a luxury tax on teams.

When the lockout was lifted on December 8, 2011, the new schedule compressed games tighter than ever before and shortened training camps. The season was going to start the day after Christmas and would feature 66 games for each team instead of the usual 82. This gave an advantage to teams with chemistry that had worked together for a long time, which, unfortunately, did not apply to the rebuilding Wizards.

What was worse for the Wizards was that even if they had already had a chance to improve team chemistry, they were still going nowhere with the players they had on the roster. Wingman Nick Young had a lot of talent but did not quite make the best decisions on the court, especially with his shot selection. Versatile big man Andray Blatche could do damage from anywhere on the floor, but his temper and demeanor always got the better of him. Center JaVale McGee had the physical and athletic qualities to become a productive player in the NBA. However, he was often caught sleeping on plays, and it seemed like his mind was wandering off elsewhere. And though Rashard Lewis was a former All-Star who had been to the Finals, his large contract held the Wizards down when attempting to sign free agents. Moreover, the other Wizards players were just too young to make an impact on the floor. Indeed, John Wall was their only bright spot.

However, John Wall would also face struggles. Wall's sophomore season was a slight disappointment. In the first game of the condensed season on December 26, 2011, Wall struggled to get 13 points after making three out of 13 field goals – most of his points came from the seven out of 13 free throws in addition to eight rebounds, five assists, and three steals. The rest of the team struggled to score in a 90-84 loss to the New Jersey Nets.

Wall did have a better game with 20 points, making six out of 15 field goals to go along with six assists and three steals, but the Wizards would struggle offensively as a group in a 101-83 loss to the Atlanta Hawks on December 28, 2011. While the team did not win the first two games, things were looking up for Wall. However, he had some scoring issues despite having some games in double-figures and a few double-doubles.

On December 30, 2011, Wall scored only six points from just getting one out of nine field goals and converting on all four free throws in a 102-81 loss to the Milwaukee Bucks at the Bradley Center in Wisconsin. This would not be the only time Wall would fail to score 10 or more points in a game. In fact, Wall would score only two points in two games on February 1, 2012, in a 109-103 loss to the Orlando Magic, and again on April 9, 2012, in a 113-85 loss to the Charlotte Bobcats. Throughout the rest of the season, Wall would score nine points twice, eight points three times, seven points twice, and four points once.

While there were a lot of negative games for Wall's sophomore season in the NBA, there were many great performances where you could see the potential the young basketball star had after having another 16 double-doubles throughout the shortened season. Fifteen of these were thanks to his ability to get the ball to his teammates for good scoring opportunities, even if that meant he was not going to pad his scoring stats as in the game against the Detroit Pistons, 98-77, on February 12, 2012, at the Palace of Auburn Hills, Michigan.

While Wall only had nine points on his three field goals and three free throws, his 15 assists were enough to help his fellow Wizards JaVale McGee and Trevor Booker score 22 points each. Bench players Jan Veselý and Rashard Lewis each had 10 points of their own to help Washington in what was just their sixth win of the season. A few weeks later, Wall would have another game with 15 assists in a close 119-118 loss on the road to the Milwaukee Bucks on February 28, 2012. Wall was able to score 19 points in the game as one of six Wizards with double-figure scoring. Trevor Booker scored 20 points, Wall and Jordan Crawford got 19 points, Chris Singleton had 16 points, Maurice Evans had 15 points, and Roger Mason had 14 points of his own. However, they were walloped by Milwaukee's Mike Dunleavy with 28 points, 15 of which came from behind the three-point line.

In addition to the high number of assists he had accumulated in his second NBA season, he also came close to a few triple-doubles. On January 20, 2012, Wall kept the Wizards close in a 108-104 loss at home to the Denver Nuggets. This was thanks to 13 points, ten assists, and nine rebounds as support for Nick Young's 25-point game and Crawford's 18 points coming off the bench. On February 22, 2012, Wall had 21 points on one of his best shooting nights (8 out of 15) to go along with 11 assists and nine rebounds in a 115-107 home loss to the Sacramento Kings. The only game where Wall had double-figure rebounds was on January 22, 2012, in a 100-94 home loss to the Boston Celtics with ten rebounds to go along with his 27 points and seven assists.

Wall would surpass the 30-point mark three times that season in front of the faithful Wizards fans at the Verizon Center in Washington, DC. This was highlighted by his 38 points from 13 out of 22 field goals and 12 out of 16 free throws in the Wizards' 114-106 loss on January 16, 2012. Wall also had 33 points in 43 minutes after making 13 out of 25 field goals and seven out of 10 free throws in a 102-95 loss to the Orlando Magic, and another 31 points from 10 out of 18 field goals and 11 out of free throws in a 111-108 home victory over the Toronto Raptors. He nearly had a couple more games of hitting that mark with two 29-point games on February 8, 2012, in a 107-93 loss to the New York Knicks, and again on February 14, 2012, against the Portland Trail Blazers in a 124-109 win.

Despite his work over the summer, Wall's jumper got worse. He only hit three three-pointers over the entire 2011-2012 season. However, he did have the sense not to take many three-point shots given how poorly he performed in that department. His first made basket that came from behind the three-point line was on January 28, 2012, against the Charlotte Bobcats. He would get another on February 14, 2012, against the Portland Trailblazers, and a third on March 26, 2012, against the Detroit Pistons.

Through the good and the bad games with Washington, Wall compensated somewhat for his worsened jumper by learning to finish around the rim, but his sophomore season was much the same as his rookie season. No one called Wall a bust since he was the only Wizard to score more than 1,000 points over the season. Wall also held averages of 16.3 points and eight assists, which were excellent for a starting point guard. He also had a 42.3 field goal percentage throughout the season, most of which came in and around the paint. However, he was not viewed favorably after he was once magnified by his selection for the 2012 All-Star Rising Stars Challenge. TNT broadcasters and NBA icons Shaquille O'Neal and Charles Barkley selected the best young players in order from best to worst. Wall was ranked 12th out of the 20 choices to Barkley's Team Chuck behind guards like MarShon Brooks, Jeremy Lin, and Ricky Rubio.

Wall would have an excellent individual performance with 17 points in his 27 minutes thanks to making 8 out of 13 field goals to go along with eight assists, six rebounds, and two blocked shots to play a supporting role coming off the bench. Kyrie Irving of the Cleveland Cavaliers led the game with 34 points as Team Chuck defeated Team Shaq 146-133 on February 24, 2012, at the Amway Center in Orlando, Florida. That seemed to be the only fun that John Wall had that season because he and his Wizards slumped all year long. They would win a total of only 20 out of 66 games they played that season.

After the All-Star break, the Washington Wizards were never close enough to fight for a spot in the playoffs. While youth was a significant factor in their inability to win games, one of the main reasons remained to be Wall's lack of considerable growth from his rookie season. He continued to struggle shooting from the field while still maintaining his status as one of the leaders in turnovers. Stat-wise, his rookie season might have even been better than his second in the NBA.

Despite that, John Wall and the Washington Wizards showed flashes of how good of an NBA team they could be in the future as the season came to an end. The Wizards never lost a game in their final six games of the season. That included wins against the Chicago Bulls and two against the Miami Heat, who were both top teams in the East. In five of those games, John Wall had double-digit assists to end his disappointing sophomore campaign on a high note.

Conquering the Slump, Injury Season

Looking back, there were some positive moments in Wall's second season in the NBA. Wall scored a career-high of 38 points against the Rockets, and Washington's winning percentage improved slightly from 28 to 30 percent with a final record of 20-46, enough for fourth place in the Southeast Division. Despite that, Wall knew that he had a lot of work to show that he was a star in his junior season. Randy Wittman, who replaced Flip Saunders after the Wizards started 2-15 in the 2011-12 season, was hoping to build on an 18-31 record as an interim.

The Washington Wizards also went through a massive roster overhaul concerning the key pieces surrounding John Wall. Andray Blatche, their leading scorer two seasons before who had barely played last year, moved over to Brooklyn to join the recently relocated Nets. Despite his versatility, he was immature and hot-tempered. Athletic center JaVale McGee had a lot of hops in his game, but his lack of focus on the court forced the Wizards to ship him over to Denver in the last season's trade deadline. Finally, Nick Young, who led the Wizards in shot attempts and ill-advised plays, was also moved to another team during the preseason. The dismissal of those three players along with the hiring of a new coach marked the beginning of a new dawn for the Washington Wizards.

The departure of the three talented yet burdensome players from the Wizards' lineup meant that the team was solely under John Wall's leadership. Realizing that he needed to improve his game, which had been stagnant over the past two seasons, Wall would follow the footsteps of Derrick Rose and Russell Westbrook, who had both developed into more than just athletic demons, but perennial All-Stars and Team USA mainstays.

Rob McClanaghan, a pro basketball trainer, was known mainly for his work in helping improve the respective games of Derrick Rose and Russell Westbrook. He was an essential part of Rose's development into a league MVP. For Westbrook, McClanaghan helped the young point guard harness his speed and athleticism to turn himself into an All-Star. Knowing that he had the same size and athleticism as both

Rose and Westbrook, John Wall called McClanaghan during the interim period before the upcoming season for the latter's services.[v]

McClanaghan was frank with John Wall. He told the developing and promising point guard that he needed a full commitment to make things work and to take Wall's game to the next level. Realizing that he was the only player that could save the Wizards' future and knowing how valuable of a player he was for his team, Wall obliged to whatever McClanaghan was going to demand from him to become a better player.[v]

John Wall's timing in seeking out the trainer's services could not have come at a better time. Back in April of the previous season, Derrick Rose was trying to recuperate from an injured knee, which prevented him from playing his best and training with McClanaghan. On the other end, Russell Westbrook was too busy leading the Oklahoma City Thunder deep into the playoffs. Wall had Rob McClanaghan's full attention since his Wizards did not qualify for the postseason.

Wall would spend the offseason in Los Angeles working with Rob McClanaghan for an hour a day at seven in the morning. McClanaghan knew what kind of a speed demon John Wall was, but helped him realize how to alternate his speeds during certain periods of the game. He also worked with Wall's jump shot, similar to how he had helped Derrick Rose and Russell Westbrook hone their respective perimeter games into deadly weapons in the NBA. With Wall,

McClanaghan taught him how to be more confident with his jump shot since defenses often sagged off on him.v

Regarding his speed, McClanaghan told Wall that he could not just blow by people in the NBA with his superior quickness. Though not many defenders could keep up with Wall in the NBA, defensive tactics had become smarter and better suited to guarding faster opponents compared to when the former Kentucky point guard was in college. McClanaghan would develop Wall's ability to change paces and speeds in the middle of the game rather than having him go full speed for the entire 48 minutes.v

With a much-improved game and confident jumper heading into the new season, John Wall set his eyes on a brighter year for himself and the Washington Wizards. He had become better and more mature in the offseason and had also grown to embrace his role as the franchise player of the Wizards. A franchise player would always want to improve on his weaknesses, and that was exactly what Wall did over the long offseason break.

Unfortunately, while Wall showed how important he was to the Wizards in his third year, it was not so much from his play as from his lack of play. Over the summer of 2012, the Wizards believed that they were ready to make a playoff run. On his part, Wall thought he could also lead his team to greater heights, especially with the work he had put in over the summer. They drafted elite shooter Bradley Beal with the third pick in the 2012 draft. Likewise, they took swingman and former NBA champion Trevor Ariza as well as two good big men in Nene and Emeka Okafor.

Unfortunately, right before the NBA preseason began, Wall was diagnosed with patellar tendonitis, a knee injury that can lead to far more serious injuries like a patellar rupture if not treated properly. He had been experiencing discomfort in his left knee, which had the Washington Wizards worrying about the health of their franchise player. Luckily, Wall was quick enough to have it checked.[vi]

Fortunately, the stress on his knee was not traumatic since it was still in its early stages. Had Wall braved through the pain and just brushed it off, the pressure would have gotten worse, and in a worst-case scenario, might have derailed John Wall's career, or at the very least, robbed him of the speed and athleticism he relies upon. Because the injury was still in its early stages, Wall was only required to rest and rehabilitate his knee without the need for surgery.

Washington announced that Wall would be out for at least eight weeks, but eight weeks later, Wall was nowhere ready to come back to the court. When Wall began skipping the pregame shoot-a-rounds shortly after his supposed return deadline, there were fears that he would have to miss the entire season to heal his knee.

The news that John Wall would have to rest some more added insult to injury in the Washington Wizards' hopes of breaking through that season. It was also a downer for Wall, who had expected himself to make a jump to All-Star status after the work he had gone through in the offseason. He had also hoped to become the leader that the Wizards needed to at least contend for a playoff spot.

The injury was catastrophic for the Wizards because they did not have a real point guard backup for Wall. They were forced to make do with bit-players like Shelvin Mack and AJ Price. The result was a disaster, especially when Nene also missed the first 11 games of the season. Even with the additions of Beal and Ariza, the Wizards had their worst start in franchise history, losing their first 12 games. By the time 2013 rolled around, their record was at 4-26, the worst in the entire NBA. Wall would finally make his season debut after the Washington Wizards' first 33 games of the season with only five wins to show for their efforts.

The plan was to ease him back into the action of the NBA after not playing for over three months. Wall came off the bench for his first several games and averaged only 26 minutes in January. In his first official game back on January 12, 2013, Wall scored 14 points after shooting 45.5% from the field (5 out of 11) in just under 21 minutes. The Wizards were able to defeat the Atlanta Hawks at home, 93-83, in front of a Washington crowd that was happy to welcome back their team's point guard. Wall also came off the bench in the Wizards' biggest blowout victory of the season with a 120-91 win over the Orlando Magic on January 14, 2013. In this game, Wall scored 12 points and collected six assists in just under 20 minutes. Wall would also get his first double-double of the season in his third game back from injury during a 95-94 loss on January 16, 2013, while visiting the Sacramento Kings. He ended the night with 14 points and ten assists as well as three steals on defense in about 26 minutes of action.

Wall steadily played more minutes as his knee grew stronger. He would play for more than 30 minutes on January 19, 2013, in a 94-87 loss to the Los Angeles Clippers (24 points and six assists) and played around 36 minutes per game in March and April. By that time, Wall was starting to reach his full capabilities on the basketball court, and one of his best statistical runs with the Wizards. His best game of his career came during the Wizards' 107-94 win at home on March 25, 2013, over the Memphis Grizzlies where he scored 47 points in less than 45 minutes. This was a result of making 13 out of 22 field goals (including two out of four from behind the three-point line) and converting 19 out of 24 free throws. Wall also collected eight assists, seven rebounds, one steal, and even blocked a shot on defense. Wall also had three games above the 30-point scoring mark, including 37 points after having 64% from the field during a 104-85 win over the Indiana Pacers on April 6, 2013, near the end of the season.

What was a very impressive statistic for Wall in the 2012-2013 season was that despite playing more than 20 games less than in his second season, he had almost as many double-doubles during his third season (14). That is because as the Wizards' point guard, Wall continued to pass the ball to his teammates to set up great scoring opportunities, which he had done since he was that high school star from Raleigh, North Carolina.

Back on March 22, 2013, Wall's distribution was an essential part of a 103-100 win on the road against the Los Angeles Lakers with 16 assists to help five of his teammates reach double-figures, including 25 points from Ariza and 15 points from Hilario. Wall also scored 24 points on 47.4% shooting from the field in that game. He also nearly helped the Wizards get a rare road victory over the Cleveland Cavaliers with a 95-90 losing effort on March 12, 2013, where Wall had 14 assists to go along with 27 points and seven rebounds.

With Wall back and the point guard position bolstered, the Wizards began to win games with "W's" in their first two games when Wall returned. In February, the Wizards had a 7-4 record and even beat some of the better teams like Denver, New York, and the Los Angeles Clippers. The Wizards even managed to make a decent push at the playoffs in the second half of the season. However, they had fallen too far behind while Wall was recovering from his injury.

John Wall's impact was shown by the vast disparity in Washington's record while he was injured compared to when he returned. They were 5-28 without Wall and 24-25 with him. Had Wall not missed so many games, the Wizards could have possibly made the NBA playoffs for the first time in five years. The Wizards finished with a 29-53 record to close out the 2012-2013 season, which was sadly their best record since 2008. However, it was still good enough to finish third in the Southeast Division and about nine games behind the eighth and final seed in the Eastern Conference playoffs, which went to the Milwaukee Bucks (38-44).

Despite not being able to lead his Washington Wizards to a competitive year like he wanted to in the offseason, it was in March of 2013 when John Wall began to show flashes of the future superstar he was to become. He would score in double digits in all of the games he played that month while also turning in some of the best performances of his career.

The best game that John Wall had played all season long was against the Memphis Grizzlies on March 25, 2013. In that career match, Wall was practically everywhere, scoring, rebounding, and assisting at will. Often criticized for his inconsistent shooting, Wall shot 13 out of 22 from the field in that game while draining 2 of his four three-point attempts and 19 of his 24 charity shots. The result was a career-high 47-point performance together with seven rebounds and eight assists for John Wall.

John Wall joined an elite group of players like Michael Jordan, Larry Bird, LeBron James, Dwyane Wade, and former teammate Gilbert Arenas to post similar statistics in the past 28 years of the league. After that performance, Wall would credit his career game to the work he put through during the summer and the efforts Rob McClanaghan exerted on him.[vi]

Wall did not have an impact by just being better than the flotsam that had manned the point guard position while he was injured. Even though he played only 49 games, those 49 games were the best of his career as he became an even more efficient scoring point guard.

Overall, Wall averaged a career-high 18.5 points per game, as well as 7.6 assists and four rebounds. He shot a career-best 44.1% from the floor, as he had grown to become more comfortable and confident with his jump shot. His third year had been marred by injuries, but Wall hoped to return to the 2013-2014 season ready to lead Washington to the playoffs.

First All-Star Season, Trip to the Playoffs

While John Wall proved that he could take his game to the next level with the improvements he showed in his third year in the league, his fourth year during the 2013-14 season was going to be his most defining as an NBA star. But for Wall, just being a breakout star was not enough. His game still had a few rough edges that sorely needed polishing.

As was shown in the few games he played during the 2012-13 season, John Wall's jump shot was thoroughly polished. Especially during his tear in March of 2013, Wall's shooting form had more consistency to it. He had learned to use his athleticism to get off shots at the apex of his jump. The numbers would prove how improved his shot was. After barely hitting 30% from three feet and above, Wall's accuracy from that distance was close to 40% in his third year in the league.[vii]

Though he had grown exceptionally in the shooting department, the question was whether he could sustain that kind of pace. John Wall, who was so used to his old shooting form, might someday return to his bad habits. And his numbers may have improved, but his shot selection still needed work. What prevented him from maturing his perimeter game was his inability to get good shots on the perimeter because most of his shots were during bailout situations or when he could not create enough space to separate himself from his defender. And while his shooting may have improved, he still needed a lot of work before he could become a deadly perimeter marksman.[vii]

And even if John Wall could perfectly hone his perimeter shooting, the question of whether he would fall in love with that part of the game arose. With his speed and athletic abilities, Wall was built to be a slasher and finisher. That was what was supposed to be his primary offensive role. The need for him to become an excellent shooter was so that defenders would not sag off on him and prevent him from driving to the basket. Perimeter shooting was supposed to be just a secondary weapon for John Wall, who still needed to find the right balance between pulling up from outside the paint and driving to the basket for easy layups.[vii] With that, Wall would continue to work on his shooting over the summer while that aspect remained to be the biggest hole in his offensive game.

Before the 2013-2014 season began, the Wizards, confident in Wall's future as an NBA star, inked him to a maximum extension of five years for $80 million. Many fans and sportswriters alike were surprised by the move. It was true that Wall had potential, but how far had Wall truly led the Wizards so far? They had failed to make the playoffs in his first three years. Although he had played the last 49 games of the 2012-2013 season without any further knee issues, a knee can betray an athlete at any time. Washington's decision to give Wall the extension now as opposed to waiting for the summer of 2014 was surprising to those who believed that they should have waited until the next summer. Such a decision showed that the Wizards were fully committed to Wall and expected him to lead them back to the playoffs.

In the first game of the 2013-2014 NBA season, Wall picked up right where he left off with a double-double on October 30, 2013, against the Detroit Pistons on the road. He garnered 20 points and 11 assists despite the 113-102 loss to Detroit. It took a little time for Wall to start getting along with Washington's latest acquisitions, which included Marcin Gortat and Al Harrington. Their first win on November 6, 2013, against the Philadelphia 76ers, showed Wall scoring 24 points with 50% shooting from the field with nine assists and three more steals on defense for a near-double-double. Wall's assists were able to help others score, and all five Wizards starters and two players from off the bench scored in double digits. He would have his best offensive performance of the season with 37 points, shooting 15 out of 21 field goals to go along with six rebounds during the team's 96-88 loss to the Toronto Raptors on November 22, 2013.

Wall responded to the higher expectations by taking his game to a new level. His decision-making improved, his three-point shot finally became decent, and his defense for a point guard remained stellar. Wall had always been capable of driving to the rim at will with his stellar speed and athleticism. But while he would have gone for a difficult layup in the past, Wall kicked the ball out to his teammates for open jumpers more often.

There were two games where Wall would match his career-high mark of 16 assists in a 104-100 home victory over the Minnesota Timberwolves on November 19, 2013. He had 14 points, five rebounds, and two steals. He did this again on March 1, 2014, in a 122-103 win over the Philadelphia 76ers. While Wall had 17 points of his own, his assists helped his teammate Ariza score 40 points to lead everyone in the game.

On January 15, 2014, the Wizards thrashed the defending champions, Miami, with a final score of 114-97. At one point, the Wizards led by 32 points in one of the most dominating efforts by Washington since 2008. Wall had 25 points and nine assists in the effort as well as two blocked shots on the defensive side of the court. A week later against the Boston Celtics on January 22, 2014, Wall had his second career triple-double with 28 points, ten assists, and 11 rebounds in a losing effort, 113-111. Near the end of the season, Wall would have his third career triple-double in a losing effort to the Charlotte Bobcats, 94-88, on April 9, 2014, garnering 14 points, 12 rebounds (11 on defense), and 11 assists in a little more than 42 minutes of playing time.

On February 16, 2014, Wall was nominated for his first NBA All-Star Game, which was played at the New Orleans Arena in New Orleans, Louisiana. While Wall only played for 15 minutes off the bench, he scored 12 points after making five out of seven from the field and had five rebounds, four assists, and two steals to support Cleveland's Kyrie Irving's 31 points as the Eastern Conference defeated the Western Conference, 163-155. Wall also helped the East win the Slam Dunk Championship on February 15, 2014, as a team before getting the overall title of "Dunker of the Night" via a vote. The nomination was thanks to a dunk where he jumped over the head of the Washington Wizards mascot and pumped the ball before slamming it in. It was a great weekend that helped propel Wall to assist the Wizards for the rest of the season.

John Wall's barrage of great performances would not end just because he had reached his goal of becoming a legitimate star in the league. Right after the All-Star break, he would lead the Wizards to six straight wins until the end of February. He had three double-doubles while tying his career high in assists in three of those stretches of wins. He also had a 31-point output in an overtime win against the Toronto Raptors on February 27.

John Wall's improvement from the three-point line had also become more evident. He made five triples out of 10 attempts against the Portland Trailblazers on March 20. He scored 24 points and assisted on 14 baskets in that loss. Nevertheless, he proved that he was not someone you could dare to shoot from beyond the arc because he had become better from that range.

Wall would come back strong in his next game by posting 28 points and 14 assists again in a win against the Los Angeles Lakers. And though it came at a loss for the Washington Wizards, the All-Star point guard John Wall recorded his second triple-double of the season on April 9, just when the season was nearing its end. He had 14 points, 12 rebounds, and 11 assists that game.

Wall and the Wizards continued to play hard in their push for the playoffs, and the team finished with a 44-38 record, good enough for second place in the Southeast Division behind the defending champions the Miami Heat (54-28), and the fifth overall seed in the Eastern Conference. Unlike the previous three seasons, the end of the regular season did not spell vacation for John Wall because he had finally made it to the playoffs for the first time in his four-year career as the designated franchise player of the Wizards.

Wall averaged 19.3 points and 8.8 assists for the year, both career highs. He also had a total of 29 double-doubles for the season with his two triple-doubles while starting all 82 games of the regular season. While Wall did not make the All-NBA team for the 2013-2014 season, no one could deny that Wall had an incredible season in his fourth year in the NBA as he helped the Wizards to their first playoff berth in several years.

The playoff berth was due in large part to how John Wall had matured as a player and a leader. Regarding his growth as a player, the most glaring improvement to his game was, of course, his shooting. Going by the percentages, Wall's shooting from the two-point area improved to a then career-best 46%. His three-point marksmanship also went up to 35% after never going above 30% in his previous three seasons.

John Wall's improvement from the three-point range was not a function of him taking fewer shots from that area. He had grown comfortable and confident in shooting as many three-pointers as he could if given the space and the occasion to shoot it. In fact, Wall's the number of three-point attempts he had in his fourth season surpass the total shots he put up from a distance in his first three seasons. He attempted a total of 308 three-point shots that season compared to the 202 he took in his first three years combined. He only shot 45 attempts from that distance the previous season. He made 108 of the 308 attempts he put up.

The improvements to John Wall's game and his growth in the shooting department were big factors in his climb towards getting named an All-Star in the East. However, more important than that was how he led the Wizards to the playoffs, not only with his improved skills, but also with an aspect often overlooked, but never understated, especially for a point guard like John Wall. He had become not only an All-Star but also a mature leader.

As John Wall would say it, he was forced to become the chief of the Washington Wizards. Fortunately, he obliged. It was during a rough start to the season when the team veterans like Trevor Ariza and Nene organized a group sit-down. After stating their frustrations about team chemistry and individual tendencies of the younger players, the floor was suddenly given to John Wall.[viii]

With the spotlight on John Wall, who was sitting in the hot seat, team veterans and youngsters alike suddenly asked his opinion on what they should be doing or not be doing as a team. Because Wall was given the designated max contract of the Wizards, everybody on the team knew who their franchise player was. Nene would tell Wall to stand up in the middle and tell everybody their roles because despite being a veteran that had been through many tough playoff battles, he knew that Wall was the franchise star that would dictate where the team was going.[viii]

From then on, Wall knew where his place was and what he needed to do. He underwent a quick maturity process from the youngster that danced through fun and exciting moments in games to an All-Star point guard that dictated where his teammates should be on the floor and what kind of tempo and pace they should be playing. And while the max contract he received during the offseason was an invitation for him to slack off and remain stagnant as a player and leader, John Wall grew into the role of a franchise star thanks to the push his teammates gave him.

In that season, John Wall had experienced what it felt like to be a legitimate NBA star. He saw his first All-Star Game while participating fairly well in the other events and festivities. He had finally won more games than he lost and made the playoffs for the first time in his career. However, Wall's goals were not going to stop at becoming an All-Star and making the playoffs. In the NBA, the ultimate prize will always be hoisting that Larry O'Brien Championship Trophy. With the performance that he and his Wizards put up that season, Wall was in good shape to make a deep run in the postseason.

In the first round of the 2014 NBA playoffs, the Wizards were set up to play against the Eastern Conference's third-seeded Chicago Bulls. Chicago was a gritty, defensive team under Coach Tom Thibodeau and had the Defensive Player of the Year, Joakim Noah. Star point guard Derrick Rose, who, like Wall, had played for Coach Calipari back in 2008, was out with continued injuries. But Chicago remained the heavy favorites because of their defensive ability and home-court advantage.

With the Chicago defense focusing on John Wall, the new All-Star point guard did not have a stellar playoff debut in Game 1. He was forced into tough shots and contested attempts, which resulted in a poor 4 out of 14 shooting clip from the field. He scored 16 points and dished out six assists in that tough opening game. Luckily, the veterans picked up the slack to steal Game 1 from the home team.

Game 2 was more of the same for John Wall. The backcourt combination of Jimmy Butler and Kirk Hinrich had the size, athleticism, and experience to frustrate Wall into taking the toughest shots possible. For the second game in a row, he struggled to shoot from the field, going 6 out of 15. Wall had 16 points, five rebounds, and seven assists in that game. However, it would take a combined effort from the team to bail the Washington Wizards out in the fourth quarter and finally win it in overtime.

Having defeated the Bulls in Chicago in the first two games to go up 2-0 in the series, John Wall and the Wizards were full of confidence heading into Game 3. Despite Wall scoring 23 points and seven assists at home at the Verizon Center on April 25, 2014, Chicago managed to win in Game 3 in Washington, 100-97, though the All-Star point guard was finally able to shake off the physical brand of defense the Bulls put on him.

However, Wall would bounce back to get his first playoff double-double with 15 points and ten assists as the Wizards defeated the Chicago Bulls on April 27, 2014, even though he was still showing signs that he was struggling against the defensive masterpiece that the Bulls played on him. He did, however, play the decoy well while making sure his other teammates were ready to pick up the slack. Ariza scored 30 big points while backcourt mate Bradley Beal contributed 18.

Game 5 would be a defensive battle at the United Center in Chicago as the Wizards defeated the Bulls 75-69 to clinch the first-round series – Wall would score 24 points and collect seven rebounds and four assists. How did the Wizards pull off the upset? Did Wall take over the series against such a great defensive team and score 30 points every night?

No, he did not. His highest scoring game was 24, and he shot 36% for the series. However, that does not mean that he had a mediocre series or that he was overwhelmed with making it to the playoffs for the first time. He was extremely aggressive against Chicago, improving his steals as well as the number of times he went to the free throw line. He also turned the ball over less, an essential factor because Chicago depended heavily on grabbing turnovers to get easy baskets. A star does not always need to take over the game or hit clutch shots. If he makes good decisions throughout an entire series, that is of greater value than a single buzzer-beater at the end of the day.

The second round of the Eastern Conference playoffs put the Wizards up against the top-seeded Indiana Pacers, who had finished the season with 56 wins and were led by a combination of Paul George, David West, and George Hill. But the Wizards had some veteran experience on their team, and that helped them in the series' first game as Washington won 102-96 on May 5, 2014, at the Bankers Life Fieldhouse in Indianapolis, Indiana. Wall may have only scored 13 points on less than 30% shooting from the field, but he also had ten assists, which helped Bradley Beal score 25 points, Trevor Ariza 22 points, and Nene Hilario's score of 15 points. John Wall was up against another tough defensive team that could probably have been the best in that department that season.

The Pacers would return the favor in the second game of the series with a hard-fought 86-82 victory on May 7, 2014. The Pacers were led by Roy Hibbert's 28 points and nine rebounds. Wall struggled on the other side of the court with only six points, making only 2 of 13 field goals attempted to go along with eight assists. The Washington offense struggled when the series brought Game 3 to DC as the Pacers took the 2-1 series lead in a dominant 85-63 decision on May 9, 2014. While Wall had 15 points, he had trouble with ball possession and had more turnovers than he did assists, which was a rare occasion. He had seven turnovers compared to his six assists. The Pacers would extend that series lead to 3-1 after a 95-92 win on May 11, 2014, in Washington – a game where Wall had issues converting with only 12 points after shooting 36.4 percent of his field goals in Game 4.

However, the Wizards were resilient to the end of the season by taking Game 5 in Indianapolis with a 102-79 victory on May 13, 2014, with Wall scoring 27 points with 11 out of 20 of his field goals going in, including three out of six shots from behind the three-point line. He also had five rebounds and five assists to help Gortat lead the team with 31 points. Many people started to think the team was gaining the upper hand in another upset of a Central Division team, but the Pacers would close out the series 4-2 after defeating the Wizards 93-80 at the Verizon Center. Wall could not replicate his Game 5 performance with only 12 points and eight assists in the season-ending loss.

Despite the great regular season, Wall struggled overall in his first appearance in the NBA playoffs after making only 36.6% from the field (21.9% from beyond the three-point arc) while averaging 16.3 points, 7.1 assists, and four rebounds during those 11 games. It was his first playoff appearance, but his debut was not exactly as stellar as he would have hoped for.

However, nobody could blame John Wall for his lackluster performances in the 2014 NBA playoffs. His Washington Wizards went up against two of the best defensive teams in the NBA. With their perimeter defense focused on the new All-Star point guard, John Wall could not help but struggle in that 11-game postseason run he had.

Nevertheless, it was evident that he had leadership qualities that could make role players play well above their normal capabilities. Second-year guard Bradley Beal had a good time in the playoffs because defenses were more inclined towards making Wall struggle from the field. He led the Wizards in the postseason with 19 points on 41.5% shooting from the three-point line. Even Trevor Ariza, who shot almost 50 percent from the field and nearly 45% from the three-point line in the playoffs, took advantage of the attention that his star point guard was getting. To top it all off, the big man combination of Marcin Gortat and Nene also fed off the looks that opposing defenses were giving them thanks to John Wall's ability to attract attention.

The performances put up by his teammates meant that John Wall could still impact the game despite struggling from the floor. It meant that he was not merely a point guard that could lead his team to wins by scoring and making assist passes. Wall's mere presence on the floor was more than enough to affect the flow of the game for the Washington Wizards. With that, it was clear that the Wizards were only going as far as their All-Star point guard could take them.

During the summer, Wall remained active by attending a camp for the 2014 US basketball team that was preparing for the International Basketball Federation's (FIBA) 2014 World Cup that was played in Barcelona, Spain on August 30 to September 14, just before the start of the 2014-2015 season. This tournament was an automatic qualifier for the 2016 Summer Olympics to be played in Rio de Janeiro, Brazil. Wall was among the best in the NBA during the camp that was led by Duke Head Coach Mike Krzyzewski.

The preliminary team of 19 players was released on July 14, 2014, and Wall was not included in a group that featured Cleveland's Kyrie Irving, Golden State's Stephen Curry, and Houston's James Harden. When Blake Griffin of the Los Angeles Clippers had to remove himself due to back problems, Wall was named a replacement on that preliminary roster before being cut on August 5, 2014, along with teammate Bradley Beal and Atlanta's Paul Millsap. Despite being cut, the experience of being at the Team USA camp for a few months provided many benefits for Wall as he returned to Washington, DC.

Leadership in Full Effect, Second Trip to the Postseason

The past year was a great season and subsequent offseason for John Wall. The only question left was how Wall could top his improving performance from the year before as he entered his fifth year in the NBA with the Washington Wizards. Despite the massive improvements that Wall displayed in the past season, he was still a developing work in progress. He still needed to improve for his team to go further.

While John Wall's offensive game had seen a drastic rise from the previous seasons, it was clear that he still had room to grow. The one department that Wall had to improve upon was running the offense. Though he could make passes and dish dimes with the best in the league, Wall's assist numbers were not quite on par with the truly elite point guards in the league. On top of that, it seemed like the many assists he was compiling on a nightly basis for the Wizards last season still could not improve the Washington offense, which ranked only 16th in points per game. Considering how good of a passer Wall was, that was still an issue that the Wizards needed to address heading into the new season.[ix]

With Wall as the designated franchise player, everyone was okay with him having the ball in his hands for the majority of the game. He was tasked to look for shooters like Bradley Beal and Trevor Ariza, who had recently transferred to the Rockets, for open shots at the corner.

He force-fed big men Marcin Gortat and Nene for easy baskets under the rim. Although Wall's role was defined as a playmaker first before scoring baskets, he was arguably better at creating shots and putting points on the board rather than having his teammates playing their best brand of basketball. Wall needed to find a balance between scoring the ball and setting up his teammates.

Another issue that John Wall needed to address was his backcourt chemistry with rising scoring guard Bradley Beal. As the franchise player in the backcourt, Wall was tasked to have possession of the ball for the majority of the plays to either score the ball himself or create shots for his teammates. As a point guard, his role was also to facilitate the basket and set plays for the team.

However, Bradley Beal, a scoring guard, had grown too talented in creating shots. He was still at the entry level of his 20's and still had enough room to grow to become an All-Star if his talents permitted him to be one. Beal's primary role when he entered the NBA was to hit open perimeter shots when Wall found him free at the wings or corners.

But over the past two seasons, Beal had grown to become a reliable shot-maker. At times, he no longer needed Wall to set plays for him, but preferred to create on his own. Aside from being the Washington Wizards' best volume perimeter shooter, Bradley Beal had also developed to become arguably the team's best player in creating his shots. His value to the Wizards was never more evident than the performance he put up in the 2014 playoffs.[ix]

In the 11-game run that the Washington Wizards had in the most recent postseason, Bradley Beal was arguably their best player. He took advantage of the defensive attention that Wall was getting to average 19.2 points, 5.0 rebounds, and 4.5 assists while shooting 41.5% from the three-point area in the playoffs. If Bradley Beal could build on his postseason performance, he might be primed for a breakout season in Washington.

While Beal had the potential to become an All-Star, the apparent problem that would arise with his development was going to be how he and John Wall could coexist in the backcourt. Though the two guards had no beef entering the 2014-15 season, chemistry issues might develop, especially when it came to who was going to handle possessions. As we know, Wall thrived whenever he had the ball in his hands because of his ability to score and create. But Beal, on his part, had become too good to become a spot up shooter at the wings. He would also need possession of the ball to become more efficient.

But, as stated, the Wizards were John Wall's team. He was the designated franchise player and the go-to guy in Washington. The Wizards trusted him with the team despite the prevalence of veterans surrounding the All-Star point guard. He would decide whether he was going to thrive and coexist with the rising Bradley Beal in the backcourt to become one of the best guard duos in the NBA, or if he would rather just keep the ball in his hands and carry the burden of the Wizards by himself.

It did not take long for John Wall to start scoring a lot of points at the onset of the 2014-2015 season. He had 30 points on 10 of 21 from the field during the team's 105-98 win visiting the Orlando Magic on October 30, 2014, which also included 12 assists in one of 40 double-doubles in what would be one of his best seasons yet of his NBA career. He would follow that up with 31 points after making 11 out of 21 field goals and eight out of nine free throws along with ten assists, six rebounds, and three steals to help the Wizards earn some revenge over the Indiana Pacers, 96-94, in overtime on November 5, 2014.

Though Wall was scoring the ball at will in the early part of the season, it was also clear that he wanted to get his teammates involved more than ever. In the Washington Wizards' first 12 games of the season, Wall assisted on 10 or more baskets on seven different occasions. He was also the priceless piece that led to a 9-3 start for the Wizards through their first 12 outings. John Wall's intent on passing more could not be highlighted brighter than the seven-game performance he put up early in December. He had double-digit assists in all of those games, which included 16 and 17-assist nights for him. The Wizards were 6-1 in that span of games.

With the improved abilities of Wall and a Washington club that added NBA veterans Paul Pierce and Drew Gooden, there was confidence building among the Wizards, and they were finding themselves beating some of the top teams in the league a lot more consistently than before. On December 19, 2014, the Wizards defeated the Miami Heat, 105-103, on the road at the American Airlines Arena in a game where Wall had 20 points on 60% shooting from the field and collected ten assists for the double-double.

He also had another 12 assists in a 104-103 road victory over the Houston Rockets on December 29, 2014. Although Wall only made 13 points in the game, he made two clutch free throws in the final seconds to seal the victory. The young team was starting to hang with some of the best NBA veterans as well, including a 101-93 win against the San Antonio Spurs on January 13, 2015, where Wall led the Wizards with 25 points and eight assists in the upset win.

As the Wizards continued to improve, Wall was developing in other parts of his game as well. He had many games where you could see his shots from a distance getting better as the season progressed. On February 4, 2015, Wall made three out of his five shots from behind the three-point arc as part of his 24 points, nine assists, and seven rebounds in a losing effort on the road, 105-96, to the Atlanta Hawks.

A few days later on February 7, 2014, Wall would make three out of five from the long distance range while scoring 17 points and seven assists in a 114-77 win at home over the Brooklyn Nets. He would have a near triple-double about two days later when he had nine points, ten rebounds, and ten assists in a 96-80 win on February 9, 2015, over the Orlando Magic. One of his best overall shooting performances came on March 14, 2015, when Wall had 31 points, making four out of five three-point field goals and a total 9 out of 15 from the field (60 percent) to go along with 12 assists in a 113-97 victory over the Sacramento Kings.

The team was looking high at the All-Star break with a 33-21 record, primarily because of key wins against the top teams in the Eastern Conference: the Atlanta Hawks, Cleveland Cavaliers, and Toronto Raptors. One year after making his first NBA All-Star Game appearance, Wall would make a return after finishing third among the top players who received votes in the Eastern Conference, only behind LeBron James of the Cleveland Cavaliers, who had 1,470,483 votes, and Pau Gasol of the Chicago Bulls, who garnered 974,177. Wall finished with 886,368 votes. On February 15, 2015, at Madison Square Garden in New York City, an arena where Wall had many memories playing basketball, Wall would finish making 9 out of 16 field goals. This included a single three-point basket and he also finished with 19 points, seven assists, three rebounds, and two steals in an excellent performance despite the Western Conference winning the game 163-158.

His field goal percentage was also improving from the last few seasons as well, and he was very effective throughout most of the NBA season. For example, Wall made 8 out of 11 field goals from 72.7% and four of five free throws for 80% in a 21-point performance that helped the Wizards defeat one of the top teams from the Western Conference in the Memphis Grizzlies, 107-87, on March 12, 2015, in

Washington, DC. Less than a week later, Wall would make nearly 70% of his field goals – nine out of 13 – and six out of seven free throws to finish with 24 points in an 88-84 win on March 18, 2015, at the EnergySolutions Arena in Salt Lake City, Utah.

In addition to being efficient, he was also a workout for the Wizards while missing only three out of the 82 games in the regular season. Wall would play for more than 40 minutes in 11 of Washington's regular season games. This included about 48 and a half minutes on March 27, 2015, during a home game where the Wizards defeated the Charlotte Hornets 110-107 in a double overtime classic where Wall finished with 32 points with nine rebounds, six assists, and two steals. Seven of his points came in the second overtime, including the go-ahead 15-foot jumper with 10 seconds left in the game.

Wall had some problems near the end of the season after dealing with some fatigue, which is common for anyone playing so many minutes throughout the season. The fatigue caused him to miss three of the final five games of the season. Nevertheless, Washington still earned a final regular season record of 46-36 to take the fifth seed in the Eastern Conference. They were second place in the Southeast Division behind the Atlanta Hawks, who finished with the conference's best record of 60-22. A big part of why the Wizards were improving their win total was because of Wall's big season with 40 double-doubles and averages of 17.6 points, ten assists, 4.6 rebounds, and 1.7 steals while making 44.5% of his shots from the field. Add that to the fact that he also improved his shooting from behind the three-point line with 30% efficiency.

John Wall's scoring numbers this season were similar to previous one, save for the fact that he shot less from the three-point line after falling in love with distance during the 2013-14 season. The big difference in the season that saw him starting the All-Star Game was his clear unselfishness in getting his teammates involved.

Often regarded as an unselfish point guard, John Wall had struggled in finding a balance between scoring and passing over the past four seasons of his career. There were days when he was so focused on scoring the ball that he would forget about making sure that his teammates were contributing. And there were also instances where he would shy away from the opportunity to score because he was so intent on setting up his teammates.

But during the 2014-15 season, John Wall found a perfect harmony between his mentality of scoring the basketball and his talent for finding open teammates. He was still finding opportunities to score the basket himself while also dishing dimes to his teammates in the process of making the game a highlight double-double performance. He nearly led the league in assists per game; his ten assists were second only to Chris Paul's 10.2. And concerning assist percentages, Wall was also third in the NBA only behind Paul and Westbrook. Those numbers show how much of an improved point guard John

Wall had become, which was why he was an MVP contender that season.

With the numbers that John Wall was putting up in every facet of the game, one would think that those numbers belonged to the likes of the most elite playmaking point guards like Chris Paul. However, with his performance that season, Wall had aligned himself with the truly elite point guards in the league, especially with how he had become the bona fide leader of the Wizards, who were contenders for a middle playoff seed in the Eastern Conference. With his statistics and improved leadership skills, John Wall was in the MVP consideration for the majority of the season, though he would not get a vote at the end of the 82-game stretch.

Though Wall's numbers as a double-double machine on the offense were what made him truly elite as far as league point guards were concerned, it was his defense that he and his team were proudest of. John Wall had finally learned how to harness his length and athleticism to become elite on the defensive end after several years of being content with being an excellent defender. During the 2014-15 season, Wall had improved leaps and bounds to become a scary perimeter defender at the point.[x]

Even coach Randy Wittman was proud of how much his star player had accomplished on the defensive end of the floor. Wittman said that he had always preached defense to his team, but it was John Wall who truly absorbed all of his instructions on that end of the floor. Wall would often hound his man into submission using his athleticism and long arms. He would even pick his assignment at full court without showing signs of fatigue on offense. Wittman would say that John Wall was the guy that made them a better defensive team that season.[x]

As a playoff team for the second season in a row, the Washington Wizards were hoping to build on the second round loss they had suffered the previous year. Coming into the postseason, they were arguably better and more balanced than their versions a year before. More importantly, John Wall had become an even better leader and facilitator. If there was a man that could lead the Wizards to a deeper run in the postseason, it was Wall.

However, Wall struggled in the first game of the opening series against the fourth-seeded Toronto Raptors on April 18, 2015, only making 27.8% of his field goals for only 10 points to go along with eight assists and six rebounds. But the Wizards had key contributions from Pierce, who had 20 points, and Beal, who scored 16 points, in a 93-86 win to take the early 1-0 series lead in Toronto.

Wall would bounce back in the Game 2 of the series in Toronto on April 21, 2015, where he scored 26 points after shooting 50% from the field in the Wizards' 117-106 victory. Wall's 17 assists were also a key for his teammate Beal to lead the team with 28 points, and three other players to score in double-digits. Gortat had 16, Otto Porter scored 15, and Pierce chipped in with 10.

The series would head back to the Verizon Center in DC where Washington continued to build upon the momentum of winning the first two games on the road. During the 106-99 win in Game 3 on April 24, 2015, Wall had another playoff double-double with 19 points and 15 assists while five other Wizards scored in double digits. The Wizards would finish the four-game sweep with a dominant 125-94 win over the Raptors on April 26, 2015, where Wall only had to play 25 minutes but still scored 14 points off three out of five from the field and a perfect seven for seven from the free throw line.

Compared to the close series that John Wall had in his playoff debut against the Chicago Bulls a year before, his performance against the Toronto Raptors was a much better sign that he had adjusted to the physical demands of a postseason series. Against the Raptors, he averaged 17.25 points and 12.5 assists, which were what made the difference. Wall had focused on setting his teammates up more.

The team felt confident going into the second round series against their division rivals the Atlanta Hawks on May 3, 2015. Washington would take the first game of the set with a score of 104-98 thanks in part to Wall's 18 points and 13 assists in support of Beal's 28 points. The Wizards also had 19 points from Pierce, 12 points each from Gooden and Gortat, and 10 points from Porter. The team was shooting well overall with a 46.7 field goal percentage.

After that game, the world realized how different of a player John Wall had become from when he was scouted as the top draftee back in

2010. Old scouting reports would tell teams that all they needed was to give space to Wall in the half court set. And in pick and roll situations, the best thing to do was yield and go under the screen to cover the point guard's driving lanes. They were going to have to give him space to shoot from the perimeter where he was not as adept.[iv] But that was then.

In that single game against the Atlanta Hawks, and in the many compelling performances he had all season long, John Wall had proven that the scouting reports about him in his rookie year now all belonged in the trash bin. He had grown significantly in the five years he had spent with the Wizards. It was all due to the tireless work he had put on his game whenever he had the chance to do so.

The John Wall of before would have frozen in situations when his ability to drive was taken away. He would not have dared to take a perimeter jump shot, though he was given the space to do so. And if he indeed had the guts to shoot a shot from a distance, the ball would most likely not find its way through the basket. Again, that was the old John Wall.

This new version of John Wall was far better. If you gave him enough space in pick and roll situations or dared him to shoot over you, he would not hesitate to do so. And when he did attempt a perimeter shot, he had reached the point where his midrange game had become a reliable gun for him to pull out of his holster quickly. On top of it all, John Wall had also developed a floater that he could use in the lane whenever the paint got too tight.[iv] Three years before, he did not have that in his arsenal. The All-Star version of John Wall had become a nearly complete scorer.

But Wall's development of a jumper was not the icing on the cake. Wall had also learned how to properly utilize his scoring abilities in pick and roll situations to draw defenses and to set his teammates up. The old version would have been forced to a turnover precisely because he could not shoot. But since teams had been wary about his ability to hit the jump shot, Wall was able to make the assist pass to Marcin Gortat's easy baskets in the dying seconds of Game 1 to seal the win for the Wizards. As they say, Wall had become a taller and more athletic Chris Paul.[iv]

But misfortune was quick to strike. Near the end of Game 1, Wall suffered an injury that affected the rest of the Wizards' playoff momentum. Wall suffered five fractures to his left hand and wrist during the first game of the series, and it was only thought to be minor at the moment. But the injury got worse to the point that he was sidelined during the second game of the series that the Hawks took on May 5, 2015, 106-90.

The rest of the team made an effort to try to pick up for Wall in Game 3, which Washington won 103-101 on May 9, 2015. Beal led the team with eight assists, but no one scored more than 20 points. Wall would miss Game 4 where Atlanta tied the series at 2-2 after a 106-101 decision on May 11, 2015. Wall would make an effort to return in

Game 5 in Atlanta on May 13, 2015, where he played 37 minutes. However, it was evident that Wall was still hampered by the injuries to his left hand and wrist, and he only scored 15 points and collected seven assists against six turnovers in the 82-81 loss. Wall missed a three-point field goal attempt in the final seconds in a heaving attempt from 45 feet away.

Wall would step up by playing an extended 44 and a half minutes in Game 6 on May 15, 2015, in Washington, scoring 20 points despite shooting seven out of 21 from the field while collecting 13 assists to help Beal score 29 points to lead the team. But the Hawks would prove to be too hot at this point and won, 94-91, to advance to the Eastern Conference Finals, which they lost in a four-game sweep to LeBron James and the Cleveland Cavaliers. It is uncertain how the Wizards would have done if it were not for Wall's injury, but it was a common belief that the Wizards could have had a better chance to defeat the Hawks and could have given a better competition against the Cavaliers as they did during the regular season.

With the playoffs already behind the Washington Wizards, one could only wonder how John Wall and his team could have fared in the Eastern Conference Finals considering that they had the frontline size and the athletic backcourt to compete with the Cleveland Cavaliers. Moreover, their physical brand of defense would have frustrated the Cavs in a way that the Hawks could not. Best of all, they had a go-to guy in John Wall, who had the ability to take control of a game when needed.

Nevertheless, Wall and his team did not even make it past the Hawks in the second round, probably due in large part to the three games that the All-Star point guard missed in that series. Had he been completely healthy and the Wizards in full strength like they were in Game 1, Washington would have had a fighting chance to defeat Atlanta and proceed to the Conference Finals. But it was not meant to be for John Wall, who had already reached elite status that season thanks to the tireless effort he exerted to improve himself. If anything, the 2014-15 season was the 82-game coming out party of John Wall as a league superstar.

The Pivotal Season, Missing the Playoffs

With the quick and sudden rise that John Wall had in his past two seasons, it seemed as if the two-time All-Star point guard was entering the point in his career where he would be catapulted to the top of the most elite players in the NBA. It would have been similar to when Chris Paul had three incredible seasons after his breakout 2008 performance or when Steph Curry suddenly became a hot commodity in 2013 when he broke numerous three-point records. Wall experienced the same rise during the 2013-14 season and improved it during the following year. The 2015-16 campaign was going to be the season that would define the identity that he had established in the past two years.

Nobody could be faulted for having the highest expectations for John Wall coming into the new season. He has drastically improved his scoring abilities by developing from being a one-dimensional slasher during his first three seasons to being a dependable perimeter shooter in the last two seasons. And while his jumper was what made defenders respect him, the growth he had shown concerning facilitating, leadership, and maturity were the reasons why he and his Washington Wizards had made the playoffs in those two All-Star seasons. They even did enough damage to reach the second round on those two occasions.

It was like how Chris Paul broke out in 2008 to become the best point guard in the league, like how Steph Curry became a fan favorite in during the 2013-14 season, and how Russell Westbrook rose to All-Stardom in his third year in the NBA. John Wall was also expected to continue a steady increase in stardom that would soon put his name up with the best of the best, not just in his position, but in the league. What was also expected of him was that he would carry the Wizards to a seeding higher than they have ever had, and a postseason run they have not seen since the time they won the league title in 1978.

Wall had too many expectations on his shoulders entering the 2015-16 season. That was why it was widely believed that the upcoming season was going to be the most pivotal one in his short six-year career. It was also what would define his career. The Wizards would have to rely on him even more because of certain factors that might have made the team much less competitive.

Paul Pierce, who had been their safety net during the past season because of his ability to make clutch shots and become a veteran presence on the team, got out of Washington and took his cold-blooded game with him to Los Angeles to join the Clippers. Nene, who was their most productive offensive big man, was slowing down with age. Lastly, most of their other role players were new additions and young recruits.

With Pierce gone, third-year forward Otto Porter, who was yet to live up to his standing as the third overall pick back in 2013, would have to step up in place of the veteran scorer alongside defensive specialist Jared Dudley. However, nobody knew what to expect of Porter since the young wingman had just won the "Shaqtin' A Fool" MVP, which was an award given to the player with the most absent-minded plays the whole season. Porter was still developing and learning. And to fill up for the tired legs of Nene, a combination of reliable but inconsistent big men of Kris Humphries and DeJuan Blair were going to have to step up.

With all that said and done, how does that relate to John Wall's predicted pivotal season? It only meant that the 2015-16 season was going to be where his abilities and status as an elite player would truly be tested. With the departure and decline of several key veteran players, and because of the apparent inconsistency of the ones filling up for those who have moved to other teams, Wall was going to be leaned on even more than when he was carrying a team full of knuckleheads back in the early stages of his career.

Though the common knowledge was that Wall was the gear that made the Washington Wizards the playoff team they were in the past two years, there were still notions that entertained the idea that the two-time All-Star point guard was only playing well because of how his team had improved.[xi] But Wall could dispel those notions by playing at an elite level in the upcoming season. In short, the Wizards would need more from John Wall entering the 2015-16 season.

John Wall was happy to oblige to what the Wizards needed him to do. In his first game for the 2015-16 season, he instantly filled the stats sheet up. In a game against the Orlando Magic on October 28, 2015, in Florida, Wall led a one-point win for the Wizards by putting up 22 points, seven rebounds, six assists, three steals, and five blocks. He would follow up that performance with a double-double in a win against the Bucks in their next game, though the Wizards would lose to the Knicks in their home opener.

Despite performing at an elite pace at the start of the season, John Wall had an immediate problem at hand. He was trying to figure out how to get back on the pace of making a playoff seed in a growingly competitive Eastern Conference picture. The Washington Wizards did not look like the playoff team that had made the second round of the postseason for the past two years and were only 9-11 in their first 20 games. Perhaps the loss of Paul Pierce and their other key role players had hit the team hard.

Nevertheless, the Wizards still had key victories despite struggling early on. After losing four straight games late in November, Washington would beat a highly-favored Cleveland Cavaliers team to snap the Cavs' nine-game home winning streak. Of course, John Wall led the way with 35 points, ten assists, and five steals. Though it came in a loss to the lowly Lakers in their next game, he had 34 points and 11 assists to record his first ever back-to-back 30-10 games in points and assists.

Things were still the same for the Wizards in December. They only evened out their wins with their losses in that month. Despite that, John Wall was still as fantastic as he had ever been. He had 13 double-doubles in December and had eight consecutive games of performing like a scoring and assist machine until the New Year. His best performance at that juncture was when he had a career-high 19-assist game against the Sacramento Kings on December 21. That would remain his best performance concerning assists.

In January 2016, John Wall was not short of highlight performances again. He would have a then-season high of 36 points together with 13 assists and seven steals against the Celtics on January 16. It came at a loss because he missed a layup that would have tied the game. He would top that performance by pulling out every move in his bag of tricks against the historic 2015-16 Golden State Warriors team led by Steph Curry, who was then regarded as the best point guard in the league.

Going up against a smaller and less athletic point guard who was considered to be the better of the two, Wall was challenged to bring out the best of his game on February 3. He made mincemeat out of Curry's comparatively weaker defense by scoring 41 points on the reigning MVP. He made 17 of his 25 field goals, which included 3 out of 3 three-point makes, while also assisting on ten baskets.

However, Wall was unable to defend the prolific shooter, who led the Warriors to a win in that game. Curry won out in that matchup by dropping 51 big points on 11 out 15 shooting from the three-point line. While Wall was regarded as an elite defender, his ability to defend the three-point line was put into question in that game as his assignment drained outside shots on him with ease.

However, John Wall would bounce back in the biggest of ways in his next game, which was against the lowly Philadelphia 76ers. He had 18 points, 13 rebounds, and ten assists for his fourth career triple-double in that easy win for the Washington Wizards. And before entering the All-Star Weekend, John Wall would put an exclamation point on the first half of the season by winning against the New York Knicks on February 9. He had 28 points, five rebounds, and 17 assists in that game.

Though John Wall would barely fail to start the 2016 All-Star Game in Toronto as hometown hero Kyle Lowry of the Toronto Raptors beat him in the voting, Wall was one of the top picks for a reserve spot on the Eastern Conference All-Star team. With the spotlight on the retiring Kobe Bryant and on other players that played monstrously in that game, John Wall's decent 22-point outing went unnoticed as the West defeated the East in a blowout.

Shortly after the All-Star break ended, John Wall recorded his second triple-double of the season against the New Orleans Pelicans on February 23. He had 16 points, 12 rebounds, and 11 assists in that win. After dropping the next game in Chicago, Wall would lead his Wizards to a four-game winning streak to end the month of February on a high note. He had 37 points on 13 out of 26 shooting in one of those wins against the Sixers on February 29.

The four-game winning streak which had given the Wizards hope of making it to the playoffs as they were contending for the final spot with the Detroit Pistons and the Chicago Bulls would be canceled out by five straight losses early in March, to their dismay. Bipolar as it may sound, the Washington Wizards would come back to win five consecutive games to get back on track. Those five wins saw some of the best performances of John Wall in all facets.

The winning streak would start with a 43-point statement win against the Detroit Pistons, who were leading them in the team standings. John Wall had a double-double in that blowout win despite barely 28 minutes of action. He followed that up with a triple-double against the Chicago Bulls, who were also contending for the final playoff spot. Wall had 29 points, ten rebounds, and 12 assists in his third triple-double that season. Against Philly in the following night, he had 16 points, 13 rebounds, and 14 assists for his seventh career triple-double to cap off the first time he had consecutive triple-double performances. In that season alone, he had four triple-doubles. He only had three in his career before that season.

John Wall's quest to lead his Washington Wizards to a third consecutive playoff appearance had him playing out of his mind the entire final stretch of the season. Since losing to the Denver Nuggets on March 12, Wall has been putting up double-digit assist games to try and force his Wizards to continue winning down the stretch. He was trying to shoulder the entire load by scoring the ball and making sure his teammates were given open looks as well.

Despite his best efforts, John Wall could not quite lead his Washington Wizards to a record that would have made them contenders for the final playoff spot, even with five more games left on the calendar for the team. Realizing that winning the last five games of the season would catapult them to their third consecutive postseason appearance, the team finally gave their superstar the rest he rightfully deserved.

All season long, John Wall had to carry the burden of leading a depleted but resolute Washington Wizards towards contending for a postseason berth. It was going to be his defining season as a superstar. Had he been able to lead them to the playoffs again, his place as an elite would have been undisputed. Nevertheless, John Wall, who had been complaining the entire 82-game stretch about nagging injuries, particularly in both knees, never asked to sit out of a game because he was determined to lead his team towards their goal of making the playoffs again.

But after it was made clear that the goal would not be fulfilled that season, Wall had to rest. His right knee was so sore at that point in the season that it became the biggest concern of the entire franchise. They could always come back stronger the following season and make the playoffs. However, the health of their best player could never be compromised since Wall relied so much on his blazing speed and athleticism for the superstar prowess he had shown over the past three seasons.

Early in May after a month's rest, Wall had surgery on both of his knees. After recovering from surgery, he would have to undergo rehabilitation and was likely to miss the Wizards' training camp.[xii] John Wall, who had never wasted his summer breaks by training hard, had to remain stagnant for a few months, unable to put to good use the tireless effort that had made him a superstar. He averaged 19.9 points, 4.9 rebounds, 10.2 assists, and 1.9 steals during the 2015-16 season, which were all career highs for him.

Despite practically going becoming a one-man team and almost reaching the playoffs in the process, Wall was not spared of criticisms the entire season. He was reported to have entered the 2015 training camp out of shape. His lack of stamina and conditioning led critics to conclude that Wall was the reason for the harsh November that the

Wizards had to endure at the start of the season. But he could not be faulted for that considering that he had suffered a postseason injury that led to the ultimate demise of Washington to Atlanta just a few months before training camp.

John Wall was unable to make enough noise in the season that would have defined his status as one of the most elite players in the league, and not just in his position, and it was not due to a lack of effort on his part. John Wall, who had to burden the heaviest load he has ever had to carry in the Randy Wittman era of the Wizards, forced his way through injuries and pains the entire season so that he could give his team a respectable finish. And while it was disappointing to see him going with an injury and missing the entire postseason, Wall's season-long performance certainly earned the respect of the entire basketball world.

And while John Wall was rehabilitating and resting the injuries he had incurred during the long 82-game long 2015-16 season, the Washington Wizards were out there trying to make the team a lot better. They had hopes of making John Wall and the entire team happy and robust enough to do enough damage towards a postseason appearance in the 2016-17 season.

With the Oklahoma City Thunder losing to the Golden State Warriors despite leading 1-3 in the Western Conference Finals, speculations arose about the future of superstar Kevin Durant, who is a Washington native. Durant was reportedly unhappy about the recent

OKC happenings and moves, which included the ousting of his beloved coach Scott Brooks. And after ten seasons and an MVP, Durant was still without a championship ring on his finger. With that, staying in Oklahoma City might not have been in his best interests if he wanted to win a title.

With Kevin Durant in the free agency market, teams were quick to court the player who was widely regarded as the second best of his era and the best scorer in the NBA. The teams that were heading the pack were the Boston Celtics, Los Angeles Lakers, Golden State Warriors, and his hometown team of the Washington Wizards.

With a solid, though declining frontline, and a young, spitfire backcourt, the Washington Wizards' biggest hole was the small forward spot. Back in the 2014-15 season, Paul Pierce provided clutch shots and veteran leadership,but he was already old. The young Otto Porter was still too raw and inexperienced to carry that kind of a load for the Wizards. Kevin Durant filling up that spot and John Wall feeding him passes in front of the former MVP's hometown crowd was an exciting thought.

However, Kevin Durant was at the point in his career when he would want to win championships in a hurry. He declined to play for the rebuilding Lakers and the steadily-rising Celtics. He did not entertain the idea of going home to pair up with John Wall, either. In the end, KD would go to the Bay Area to sign with the Golden State Warriors, who had just won 73 games in the previous regular season, to form a super team that had a chance to become the deadliest squad ever assembled.

With KD's decision to go to the Warriors now behind them, the Wizards had to work with the pieces that they had. An important man they picked up was a new head coach, Scott Brooks, who they hired as one of the means to draw Durant in. However, the most significant move that they accomplished after the 2015-16 season was signing Bradley Beal to an extension of five years, which virtually locked him in Washington for the majority of his young and developing years. Unfortunately, the sum of the contract was not exactly good news for their franchise superstar.

John Wall was reportedly unhappy about the $130 million extension that Beal got. After all, he had only got $80 million several years back before breaking out to become an All-Star. But Beal was yet to reach stardom and has yet even to show any signs that he would reach that level anytime soon despite the obvious talent that he had. John Wall, however, wanted his backcourt mate to flourish just as he did after receiving a massive offseason extension. Despite the obvious chemistry issues with Beal, Wall wanted nothing more than to have his scoring guard breaking out in the next season to prove that he was worth $130 million.[xiii]

But for all the moves that the Wizards made in the offseason to improve on the team, the only aspect of the next season that John Wall could control was how he would play. After a pivotal season that saw him going down with an injury, Wall still had a lot of things to prove wrong. Questions arose about how he could come back healthy and with the same explosiveness after knee surgery. There were also queries about how he could adjust to Brooks' style of play and whether or not he could coexist with Beal. Answers to those doubts and questions were all within the palm of John Wall's hands, just as he believed he has his defenders at his mercy.[xiv]

Becoming Elite, the Rise of Bradley Beal

If there was anything that Randy Wittman's system showed, it was that the Washington Wizards could not thrive by being a defensive team. They had defensive talents in the likes of John Wall and Bradley Beal, who could both become lock-down defenders if they chose to. However, Wittman's system also put to waste the obvious speed advantage that John Wall had over any other guard in the league. Beal was also fast and was still young enough to outrun his defenders.

But before John Wall could even make the jump from being the leader of a slow-paced defensive team into the man headlining a fast-paced offensive attack, he first had to make sure he could run. After the offseason surgeries he had on both knees, John Wall felt like his left leg was dead because of the major procedure he had undergone.

John Wall, during the recovery process, could not even do as much as bending his left knee. It was a meticulous recovery period that made

Wall try to learn how to walk again. The first thing he had to do was learn how to bend that knee again without the pain he felt during the early parts of his recovery process. He went step by step by trying to walk properly with both legs up until he started jogging and do little movements.[xv] It was the little things that helped him recover back to his peak form.

However, things were just as difficult for John Wall on a mental aspect as they were from a physical standpoint. Wall was a player that could to athletic plays and movements that only probably a handful of other people in the world could do. He was so used to doing big moves and doing things so fast and athletically that he became a sensation. However, during the recovery process, everything was slow and tedious for him. He had to do little things that he thought were unsatisfying especially for a player like him that was so used to doing the most spectacular body movements imaginable.[xv]

For John Wall, everything unrelated to basketball during his recovery period felt devastating. He could not even swim, run, or go on the court to play the game he loved. It seemed as if he had lost all the strength he needed in that left leg of his after that major surgery.[xv] But all he could do at that point was to recover and try to strengthen his knee legs back through various exercises designed especially for him and the impending return of his explosiveness.

John Wall got back to form, and his knee had regained its strength and explosiveness. Looking back, Wall believed that the knee injury was a wakeup call and a test he had to go through at that point in his career. It was a sign for him to take better care of his body and to look after not only his legs but also the other parts of his physique to make sure that his knees were not overcompensating.

The All-Star point guard also admitted that he used to recklessly dash on the court without having to think about the damage it was doing to his legs. During the recovery period, he spent time watching old high school and college films. He saw how so much explosive he was back then not because he was younger and more athletic but because he was relying more on his physical talents more than what his skills and his basketball IQ could provide him.

Since joining the NBA ranks, John Wall has been steadily improving his game. What started out as a point guard that outdashed and outjumped the competition methodically transformed into a player that hit perimeter jumpers better on a consistent basis. He has been improving his fundamentals ever since and has also grown in maturity and basketball smarts. John Wall himself believed that the injury had helped him re-evaluate about his own game. He thought that the new version of himself would be a perfect marriage between his superhuman athletic gifts and the fundamentals and IQ he has learned to develop ever since he was drafted back in 2010. John Wall could perhaps now rise to the elite level that point guards such as Russell Westbrook and Stephen Curry have reached.

With the work he had done with Rob McClanaghan since 2013, John Wall had developed a jumpshot that became a reliable weapon for him. He started working out on 15-feet jumpers when he first collaborated with the known trainer. Then, as seasons went by, he slowly moved farther away from the basket until he became a player you could not leave from the three-point line the last season. It was John Wall's jumpshot that turned him from a one-dimensional scorer into an all-around threat on the floor.

However, John Wall believed that he was also working with bad knees the past three seasons. He may have developed a consistent perimeter game, but he has since relied more on his jumpers rather than his athleticism because of the knee injuries he has been enduring the past seasons. But coming into the 2016-17 season, John Wall had already recovered from the knee surgeries he had undergone to fix his injuries. He was positive that, with the explosiveness he has regained and the perimeter game he has developed, he could become the superstar new head coach Scott Brooks wanted him to be.

Speaking of Scott Brooks, he was widely known as the head coach that turned both Kevin Durant and Russell Westbrook into superstars at the individual level. Though he was unable to deliver a title to Oklahoma City with the degree of talent he had in KD and Russ, Brooks knew that he could also turn the Wizards' backcourt into an explosive tandem that had much more chemistry and flow compared to Durant's and Westbrook's tendencies of playing isolation basketball.

With John Wall's fiery game and his ability to play the transition coupled with Bradley Beal's expertise on catch-and-shoot situations and in moving well without the basketball, Scott Brooks knew that the Wizards had a backcourt built to run and score points in a hurry. He had the team transition from being a defensive squad into a group of players that focused on pace and transition plays. The system was perfect for John Wall and Bradley Beal, who was still in the process of proving he was worth the lucrative extension he just signed to during the offseason.

Still trying to get his legs back from the surgery, John Wall started the season slowly though he still ended up with a double-double in the Washington Wizards' opening game. On that night of October 27, 2016, Wall had 12 points and ten assists to go along with four steals. However, his team ended up losing to the Atlanta Hawks. Though John Wall had a remarkably better performance the following game three days later, he still could not carry the Wizards to a win. He finished that night with 22 points and 13 assists.

On November 2, John Wall had one the best nights he had that season. He shot 13 out of 19 from the floor to score a total of 33 points. He also dished out 11 assists to record his third straight double-double to start the season. However, he did have nine turnovers that compensated for what was an otherwise spectacular performance. In the end, the Wizards still lost that one to the Toronto Raptors to fall to 0-3.

John Wall would taste his first victory that season at the expense of the Atlanta Hawks on November 4. That night, he had 21 points, ten rebounds, and six assists to record his fourth straight double-double to start the season. It was a good enough performance to give his team their first win that season. However, Wall had to rest out the next game as the Wizards' measure of making sure his knees did not get stressed out. John Wall was scheduled to rest the second game of back-to-backs at that early juncture of the long campaign.

With John Wall still apparently trying to get back into form, the Washington Wizards struggled out of the gates early that season. They ended up losing eight of their first ten games and were looking outmatched by what was a weaker Eastern Conference. But John Wall tried to rectify it by going for a good individual four-game stretch in the middle of November.

Wall started out by going for 23 points and 11 assists against the New York Knicks on November 17 to give the Washington Wizards their third win that season. The next day, he went for a new season high of 34 points on 12 out of 25 shooting from the floor against the Miami Heat. He also only missed one of his six three-pointers that night and also contributed with eight assists. However, the Wizards narrowly missed the win. And though Wall had a difficult shooting night on November 21 against the Phoenix Suns, he still finished with a season high 15 assists before going for 26 points and ten assists in a win against the Orlando Magic four days later. During that four-game stretch, Wall averaged 25.3 points and 11 assists as the Wizards were 3-1 and were quickly gaining traction.

After starting out the first two games of December totaling 42 points and 28 assists, Wall would go for a new career high in points. On December 6 against the Orlando Magic, he could not be denied from getting his buckets. John Wall made 18 of his 31 field goals and 5 of his eight three-pointers to score a total of 52 points, which was a new career mark for him. He also had eight assists and three steals. Despite that performance, they could not escape with a win against a struggling Magic team.

Despite that loss, John Wall spectacular performances during December helped the Wizards gain some traction as a playoff contender. John Wall had several fantastic performances that month. He went for a new season high in assists when he tallied 16 dimes in a win over the Milwaukee Bucks on December 26. Then, in the game after that, he nearly had triple-double against the Indiana Pacers when he finished with 36 points, 11 rebounds, and nine assists. It was also during that month when Wall became the franchise leader in steals in only seven seasons. It happened when he collected six steals in a win over the Charlotte Hornets on December 14. Overall that month, Wall averaged 24.5 points, 4.4 rebounds, 10.7 assists, and 2.6 steals. He shot nearly 50% from the floor and also collected 11 double-doubles in a month where the Wizards went 10-5 in the 15 games they played. Because of that, he was named Eastern Conference Player for the entire month of December.

As early as the third game of the 2017 season for the Wizards, John Wall went for a new season high of 18 assists in addition to the 18 points he had against the Minnesota Timberwolves on January 6. Just four days later, he had another double-double outing by going for 26 points and 14 assists when the Wizards defeated the Chicago Bulls.

Wall would then lead the Wizards to a four-game winning streak in the middle of January. He started out with 25 points, seven rebounds, and seven assists on January 14 before going for 24 points and seven assists two days later. Then, against the Memphis Grizzlies on January 18, he had 25 points and 13 assists. He finished the streak the following night with 29 points and 13 dimes versus the New York Knicks. John Wall averaged 24 points and ten assists during that run.

Just a game after that four-game winning streak ended, Wall led the Wizards to a seven-game run. One of his best performances during that streak was when he dished out a new season high of 19 dimes against the New Orleans Pelicans on January 29. Then on February 2, he had 33 points and 11 assists against the LA Lakers. In those seven wins, Wall averaged 23 points and 11 assists.

It was also that 19-assist night against the Pelicans that started what eventually became a 19-game streak of consecutive double-doubles in points and assists. In the middle of all that, he was named an All-Star for the fourth time in his career and also tied his season and career high of 19 assists for a second time that season. He averaged 21 points and 13.6 assists during those 19 games. The Wizards lost only three games during that spectacular run by John Wall.

John Wall would perform well in a stretch of five straight wins for Washington. He had four double-doubles in that run, and the game where he narrowly missed a fifth straight double-double was when he scored 39 points in an overtime win against the Portland Trailblazers on March 11. He hit 13 of his 23 shots in that game and also dished out nine assists. During that run, he averaged 27.6 points and 11 assists.

On March 17, John Wall would exceed his career high in assists. In that win over the Chicago Bulls, he would go for 14 points and a ridiculous amount of 20 assists. Practically everyone on the Wizards' roster was clicking that night because of how Wall was finding them at every open opportunity for the highest quality of shots they could get.

In the last days of March, John Wall had great back-to-back performances against Los Angeles' two teams. He started out by going for 39 points, 14 assists, and four steals against the Lakers on March 28 in a win. The next night, he challenged the Clippers' defense by shooting 16 out of 23 from the floor for 41 points in addition to 7 rebounds, eight assists, and three steals. However, the Clippers came out the winners of that game.

As the dust settled, the Washington Wizards did well enough to secure the fourth seed in the Eastern Conference. At the helm of that charge and return to the playoffs was John Wall, who averaged career highs across the board. He averaged 23.1 points, 10.7 assists, and two steals. He also shot a career high 45% from the floor that season to prove that he had fully mastered his perimeter game and that his knee and his explosiveness were in full effect. And for the first time in his career, Wall was an All-NBA selection having been named to the Third Team. That certainly cement John Wall as an elite guard.

However, John Wall's rise as an elite superstar was not the only reason why the Washington Wizards performed better that season. A significant amount of the credit would also go to Bradley Beal, who also averaged a career high 23.1 points that season. The then 23-year-old Beal only averaged 17 points the following season in a slow-paced defensive system. He was also used strictly as a catch-and-shoot player because of his inability to create for himself.

But during the 2016-17 season, Bradley Beal showed a significant jump in his ability and efficiency in scoring. He not only increased his shot attempts but was making them at an elite rate. Beal shot 48% from the field as a perimeter scorer and also made nearly three three-pointers a night while shooting 40% from deep that season. Though he did not become an All-Star that season, he lived up to the expectations that John Wall had of him as he had finally harnessed his talents and evolved into a good scorer that not only made a high volume of his shots, but could also create for himself off the dribble.

The improved relationship between John Wall and Bradley Beal also gets credit to how fluid the duo looked the entire season. Before the season, Wall was openly critical of Beal's contract as it seemed like he did not believe that the shooting guard earned it. He also publicly said that he and Beal had a tendency to dislike each other and were not the best of friends on the court. They hardly even talked to one another outside of the realms of basketball despite the fact that they have been playing together for five years already.[xiii]

Beal himself said as much. He believed that he and Wall had trouble communicating because they were both alphas on the team. He thought that it was always going to be a tough situation when you have two guys that have supreme confidence in themselves to the point that they thoroughly believed that they were the leading man of the squad. But he also came to realize that he needed Wall just as much as Wall needed him.

While John Wall knows that he and Bradley Beal might never become the best of friends, the least they could agree on was that it was important for them to be able to hash out their individual goals and where they wanted to see themselves in the long run. For Wall, he believed that being on the same page was the key to improving the relationship he had with his backcourt sidekick.

When the season was nearing its end, John Wall admitted that he and Bradley Beal had developed their relationship by simply being on the same page. For him, every superstar duo bumped heads. He saw that with Shaq and Kobe. Durant and Westbrook did not have the best chemistry on the court. But John Wall and Bradley Beal took the next step by learning to understand that they could not be the players that they were and could not have had career seasons during that campaign if they did not help each other out in the first place. It even went as far as both players complimenting each other.[xvi]

While it was a huge boom for the Wizards that Wall and Beal were performing at career levels and had improved their relationship, more work needed to be done. To ultimately cement himself as an elite leader in the NBA, John Wall had to take the Washington Wizards to heights that the franchise had not seen in a long while. He had to take them deep into the playoffs.

John Wall's road to cement his legacy within the franchise started against the Atlanta Hawks in the first round. He made minced meat out of the Hawks' defense that night. Wall was making his shots at an efficient rate while also setting his teammates up for good open looks. He ended up with a career playoff high of 32 points in addition to the 14 assists he dished out that night to give the Wizards a 1-0 lead.

To prove that his Game 1 performance was not a fluke, John Wall ultimately repeated it in Game 2. Wall was aggressive the entire night and was making his way to the free throw line by always attacking the basket. He made 12 of the 15 free throws he attempted and scored a total of 32 points but narrowly missed a double-double after tallying nine assists that night. Once again, his play and leadership were vital in giving the Wizards a 2-0 lead.

No matter how well John Wall played in those first two games, things nearly fell apart when the series moved to Atlanta. Though Wall played well enough to score 29 points on 10 out of 12 shooting from the field in Game 3, the Hawks' offense was rolling as they defeated the Wizards by 18 points. And despite the 22 points and ten assists that the four-time All-Star point guard had in Game 4, he could not stop the Atlanta Hawks from tying the series with two wins apiece.

Back in Washington, John Wall went back to work by becoming the offensive catalyst. He dished out dime after dime to end the game with 14 assists and to regain the series advantage. He finished that night with 20 points and six rebounds as well. The Washington Wizards were merely one game away from making to the second round after missing the entire postseason a year ago.

Not willing to let the Atlanta Hawks force Game 7, John Wall went to work in front of a hostile crowd in Game 6. Despite the jeering and boos he was getting in Atlanta, Wall went for a new playoff career high in points. Wall was unstoppable and was running through a Swiss cheese Hawks defense to score 42 points on 16 out of 25 shooting from the floor. The Wizards took the series by winning Game 6 by 16 points.

Things would not get easier on the part of John Wall come the second round. While he had the clear advantage concerning size, he still had to go through the trouble of guarding the NBA's third leading scorer that season. Despite his lack of size, Isaiah Thomas was a handful of a scorer would often look too difficult to stop by any defender.

John Wall's defense was tested in Game 1. Thomas was running circles around the entire Washington Wizards team while also shooting over any defensive looks he was given. Thomas ended the game with 33 points as Wall failed to contain him. Despite that, John Wall still performed admirably after going for 20 points and 16 assists. Facing the top-seeded Eastern Conference team, the Wizards succumbed to the Celtics' home court advantage.

Game 2 was a vicious battle between two of the Eastern Conference's best point guards. It was essentially a one-on-one bout where John Wall and Isaiah Thomas were both trying to outdo the other. For the second time during the postseason, John Wall cracked the 40-point mark by going for 40 points. This time, he completed the double-double by going for 13 assists. However, Thomas did better on the scoring end by going for 53 massive points to pull the Wizards down to a dangerous 0-2 hole in the series.

Things started to click when the series shifted to Washington. The Wizards played an inspired brand of basketball in front of their home court crowd. Of course, Wall was the catalyst of that Game 3 blowout win as the Wizards showed that they were not in a fight they could not win. The point guard finished with 20 points and eight assists. Meanwhile, Game 4 was not so different considering that the Wizards were able to blow the Celtics out of the building again. Despite the shooting woes in that game, John Wall finished with 27 points, 12 assists, and five steals to lead Washington into tying the series 2-2.

Unfortunately for Wall and the Washington Wizards, the Boston Celtics would blow them out in Game 5 to setup a dramatic Game 6 finish. Often criticized for his inability to hit go-ahead jumpers, especially from the three-point line, John Wall got the ball with barely eight seconds to work with as the Celtics were up by two points and were seemingly in the cusps of eliminating the Wizards. Wall got the inbound pass near the right wing. He sized up Avery Bradley, one of the league's best perimeter defenders. Thinking that Wall was going for a drive, Bradley gave him room to operate. Then Wall suddenly rose up for a shot 26 feet away from the basket and well beyond the wing three-point line to drain a shot over the outstretched arms of his defender with a little over three seconds left.

The game ended with the Celtics unable to convert at the other end. As the buzzer sounded, John Wall hopped onto the scorer's table flexing his muscles over the Washington crowd after showing the effects of how clutch he was when it mattered and how he had improved his ability to hit three-pointers. From a player that barely took any shot from a distance during his first three seasons, John Wall had evolved into a player that would not hesitate to attempt a three-point basket when his team's entire season was on the line. The point guard finished that game with 26 points and eight assists.

John Wall and the Wizards were unable to replicate that dramatic finish in Game 7 when the Celtics defeated them by 10 points. It was a quick turn of events for John Wall, who just hit a three-pointer a few days ago to save his life. In Game 7, he fell in love with the shot but just made a single three-pointer out of the eight attempts he had. While he had shown improvement in his ability to hit that shot, he was still far from automatic and consistent from that range. He finished with 18 points, seven rebounds, and 11 assists in that game, and was unable to keep his team's hopes alive as he did back in Game 6.

With that loss, the Wizards bowed out of the playoffs but not without a valiant effort from John Wall, who averaged 27 points and ten assists the entire postseason. And if there was any consolation for the Washington Wizards, it was that John Wall has finally emerged as a superstar while his backcourt mate was slowly earning his keep as a future All-Star. If everything continues to go well in the nation's capital, the Wizards would still be a force to fear in the Eastern Conference.

Chapter 5: Wall's Personal Life

While Wall played only one year at the University of Kentucky, he continues to have a strong connection with the Wildcats and Coach Calipari. He returns to Lexington every summer to work out with Coach Calipari and stated in 2014 that he believed that Calipari could coach an NBA team. In September 2013, Wall played a charity alumni game in Kentucky's Rupp Arena alongside fellow freshmen like Patrick Patterson, Terrence Jones, and Anthony Davis. A month later, Wall and Davis, the star of the 2012 Kentucky team that won the NCAA tournament, played against each other in a preseason game. Davis' New Orleans Pelicans prevailed, but Wall talked about how great it was to return and see the swell of Big Blue Kentucky fans cheering for both of the former college stars.

Outside of basketball, Wall is a generous but prudent man who cares deeply about his family. Upon signing his first $80 million extension with the Wizards, he broke down in tears as he talked about how hard his family had worked to get him where he is today. He immediately gave $1 million away to children's charities and helped set his mother up with a house in Washington. In his free time, Wall enjoys listening to music and competing in everything he can. His choice of music, however, proved to have limitations. After listening to Bon Jovi's performance in a game against the Toronto Raptors, Wall admitted that he had no idea who he was.

In addition to his private charity donations, Wall is also part of NBA Fit, a basketball initiative that promotes healthy lifestyles and exercise across the nation. When Wall first joined the league, he regularly munched on snacks and fried food. However, he had to adjust his diet to handle the physicality of the NBA. When he injured his knee and was unable to exercise routinely, he packed on a few pounds, which prompted him to realize the necessity of eating healthy. Currently, Wall eats primarily baked food and vegetables with waffles, grapes, and a smoothie for breakfast. He also bikes in the off-season to keep himself in shape. The Wizards and Wall have partnered with several youth basketball programs in the DC-Northern Virginia area, helping to get them out onto the court and away from the television and computer. Wall also serves in the NBA's Hoops for Troops program, which seeks to reward American military members for their service. In a Wizards Salute to the Stars event, Wall, as well as other Wizards, served as celebrity members for veterans, chatting and thanking them for their courage.

Chapter 6: Impact on Basketball

John Wall stands 6'4", weighs about 200 pounds, and has a wingspan that is almost 6'10". Looking at those physical attributes, one would not dare to think that they belong to an elite point guard in the NBA. However, big point guards were never much of a rarity in the league. The NBA has seen the likes of Oscar Robertson, Magic Johnson, Jason Kidd, and Penny Hardaway, all of whom were big playmakers during their time.

However, what made John Wall more unique and intriguing than his predecessors was not his size. You have a 6'4" point guard, and that is instantly good news. Add the fact that Wall jumps off the roof and is arguably the quickest player in the NBA, and you have one of the most physically gifted point guards the league has seen in its history.

Together with the likes of Derrick Rose and Russell Westbrook, John Wall is one of the players that ushered in a new generation of fast, athletic, and scoring point guards with abilities and skills unseen before in the NBA. Never has the league been impacted so much by the athleticism and skill of a large point guard such as John Wall. He has become one of the reasons why the NBA has been dominated by point guards lately.

However, John Wall was never as bright of a star as he is today. He used to be criticized for being a one-dimensional player that relied too much on his speed and athleticism to blow by opponents and finish dunks or layups at the basket. It was widely believed that Wall was unlike his predecessors in the sense that he did not fully utilize all the natural talents that he had.

At 6'9", Magic Johnson used all of his height and length to see over defenders and make the best passes the NBA has ever seen. He also suffocated his opponents on the defensive end with his long frame. Jason Kidd, while not the most athletic point guard, used all of his smarts and size to rebound and defend like there was no tomorrow. Gary Payton, nearing 6'5", posted and bullied smaller point guards into submission while never forgetting to put the clamps on them defensively.

Today, even players near the size and athleticism of John Wall can hone their natural talents to become superstars. Derrick Rose, with his size and speed, developed an unguardable floater in the lane in case he cannot blow by his defenders. He also was able to become a respectable three-point shooter. Russell Westbrook, who used to be all about attacking the basket relentlessly, became an unstoppable scorer with his quick pull-up jump shot and his newly developed finishing moves in the lane while also growing into today's Mr. Triple-Double.

However, in the case of John Wall's early career, he did not show the same passing mentalities of Magic Johnson. He did not post smaller defenders up or make use of his lateral quickness and length to bottle them up defensively similar to how Payton did in the past. Wall did not show the instincts of being everywhere on the floor, much like Jason Kidd did, nor did he have the finishing grace of a Derrick Rose or the relentless aggression of a Russell Westbrook. John Wall did not have those qualities because he was a different player.

As John Wall learned with experience over the early course of his NBA career, the naturally-talented point guard learned how to hone his gifts and turn himself into a deadly player in the league. By tirelessly working on his jump shot, which was seen as his Achilles heel early on, Wall learned how to make defenders respect his perimeter game and made it easier for him to drive to the basket. Though still relying on his speed, John Wall realized that by developing an outside game, the driving game comes to you much easier.

Although Wall did not have the natural IQ of Magic or Kidd when it came down to playmaking, he honed his passing game as an offshoot of his overall developed offensive game and maturity on the leadership end. With his improved jumper, the pick and roll game became much easier for John Wall as his passing lanes became available. And knowing how valuable of a player he was for the Wizards, he made it a point every single night to get his teammates open as he had developed into a double-double machine for the Wizards.

And though he does not have the grace or mobility of Derrick Rose or the ruthless aggression of Russell Westbrook, Wall's growth concerning knowing when to attack or to pull-up from the perimeter were miles ahead of when he was in his rookie and sophomore years in the NBA. On the offensive end, he has become his own man.

Finally, through the tutelage of former head coach Randy Wittman, Wall has also learned how to fully utilize his length and athleticism to frustrate his smaller assignments and fill-in passing lanes for easy steal opportunities. The defensive growth that John Wall has shown since his rookie year was so palpable that he was arguably the Wizards' defensive anchor during their 2014-15 season when the team was at its best on that end of the floor.

All things said and done, John Wall's impact on the game of basketball is not solely entrenched on how he helped usher in a generation of big and athletic point guards in the NBA. It is also in how he has shown the ability to rise above his reliance on his natural physical gifts to become a solid and elite NBA star. Few players have shown such an ability.

The league has seen its share of naturally gifted players that have declined quickly after injuries hampered their superior athleticism and speed. It has also seen players, though healthy through the majority of their respective careers, who have never developed beyond their athletic capabilities and became nothing more than a shell of their former selves as they aged in the NBA. But with the way that John Wall has developed his game outside of his speed and explosiveness, we have seen how an athletic point guard could change the fate of a struggling NBA franchise. That was what John Wall's biggest impact was above all that he has given to the game of basketball.

Chapter 7: John Wall's Future

In September 2015, Wall and other stars from Kentucky joined the man who coached them to success with the Wildcats during John Calipari's induction into the Naismith Memorial Basketball Hall of Fame. Wall was one of the biggest impact players looking back at the recent years in the program. There have been many great players to be taught by Calipari between Kentucky, Memphis, and UMass. However, Wall is arguably one of the best among that group to be discussed with names like Marcus Camby, Derrick Rose, and Tyreke Evans.

For a player as young as Wall, his future can be examined both in the short term and the long term. Regardless of where Washington goes from here, Wall and the Wizards have found a lot of success, which started to show in the 2013-14 NBA season playoffs. The young man who once suffered from maturity issues has developed into a confident point guard ready to lead the Wizards, no matter how far they may go. Los Angeles Clippers point guard Chris Paul remains the best pure point guard in the NBA, and Wall is not the only young point guard seeking to take Paul's throne.

There is Derrick Rose, who has won an MVP, and Russell Westbrook, who was the second option on a championship team. Stephen Curry, who has led the Golden State Warriors out of years of irrelevancy and won a title and two MVP's in the process is a contender, despite the fact that he is more inclined towards shooting the ball than making plays. Chris Paul, who is overall the best all-around point guard in the league with his ability to put triple-doubles up in a hurry, and Damian Lillard, who has proven to be a monster in the clutch over and over again, drilling a series-clinching 3-point shot in the 2014 playoffs against the Houston Rockets.

But what about John Wall? He has the athleticism on par with a Derrick Rose or a Russell Westbrook. He has shown the ability to run an offense the same way that Chris Paul has done so through for the majority of his career. Wall has also turned into a leader like Curry is and was able to drain clutch shots in the same manner as Lillard has. But why is he not the best out of the bunch?

Many point to his lack of aggressiveness on the offensive end. Gifted with speed that could outrun a gazelle and the explosiveness that is on par with a grenade, John Wall should be able to get layups and free throw attempts with ease. However, only about 30% of his career attempts were from inside the paint, and he has only attempted about five free throws a game, a statistic that has declined ever since he has developed a perimeter jumper.

Despite the fact that Wall believes himself to be able to control his defenders one-on-one, the numbers do not necessarily show it. In his best years, Rose was attempting nearly seven free throws a night, while Westbrook could draw almost ten in the year he won the scoring championship. Even the smaller and less athletic Chris Paul draws the same amount of foul shot attempts as Wall has in his career. All those beg the question of how truly competitive and aggressive John Wall is.

Looking at Wall's skills and talents, one would believe that he has all the tools to become the best point guard in the league. However, he has not shown the mentality nor the aggressiveness to contend for that crown in the most contested position in the league. Wall's relative lack of success in the league also contributes to that.

While he has shown significant improvement during the 2016-17 season, especially with his ability to score his aggressiveness at attacking the basket, John Wall's success at the point guard position was still overshadowed by the achievements of other players at his spot. Russell Westbrook was named the MVP and averaged a triple-double the entire season. Meanwhile, James Harden, who was not even a natural point guard but was only converted into a full-time playmaker that season, led the league in assists. And lastly, Steph Curry ended the season by hoisting his second NBA championship in only three seasons. This all begs the question of where John Wall lies among the league's best point guard and how he will be able to stay on par with the elite as all the other accomplished playmakers in the NBA have either won the MVP or have finished the season as a champion.

There is no doubt in anyone's mind that John Wall has already reached elite status among the NBA's point guards. The only thing he now needs to prove his ability to take his game to another level the same way all the other superstar point guards in the league seemingly continue to elevate their performances season after season. But more importantly, what John Wall has to do is to secure his chance at an NBA title if he wants to be known as an all-time great at his position.

Can Wall truly prove himself to be the best point guard of them all? Only time will tell, and the Wizards will do their best to provide him with all the help he needs. In the seven years he has been in the NBA, he has only made the playoffs thrice. The reasons have been combinations of maturity problems, deficiencies in his skills, injury problems, and lack of equally capable All-Star teammates for John Wall. And yet, with the talent and tireless efforts that he puts himself through every season, his status concerning becoming the best point guard is not a question of why or how. It is a question of when.

Final Word/About the Author

I was born and raised in Norwalk, Connecticut. Growing up, I could often be found spending many nights watching basketball, soccer, and football matches with my father in the family living room. I love sports and everything that sports can embody. I believe that sports are one of most genuine forms of competition, heart, and determination. I write my works to learn more about influential athletes in the hopes that from my writing, you the reader can walk away inspired to put in an equal if not greater amount of hard work and perseverance to pursue your goals. If you enjoyed *John Wall: The Inspiring Story of One of Basketball's Fastest Point Guards*, please leave a review! Also, you can read more of my works on *Roger Federer, Novak Djokovic, Andrew Luck, Rob Gronkowski, Brett Favre, Calvin Johnson, Drew Brees, J.J. Watt, Colin Kaepernick, Aaron Rodgers, Peyton Manning, Tom Brady, Russell Wilson, Michael Jordan, LeBron James, Kyrie Irving, Klay Thompson, Stephen Curry, Kevin Durant, Russell Westbrook, Anthony Davis, Chris Paul, Blake Griffin, Kobe Bryant, Joakim Noah, Scottie Pippen, Carmelo Anthony, Kevin Love, Grant Hill, Tracy McGrady, Vince Carter, Patrick Ewing, Karl Malone, Tony Parker, Allen Iverson, Hakeem Olajuwon, Reggie Miller, Michael Carter-Williams, James Harden, Tim Duncan, Steve Nash, Draymond Green, Kawhi Leonard, Dwyane Wade, Ray Allen, Pau Gasol, Dirk Nowitzki, Jimmy Butler, Paul Pierce, Manu Ginobili, Pete Maravich, Larry Bird, Kyle Lowry, Jason Kidd, David Robinson, LaMarcus Aldridge, Derrick Rose, Paul George, Kevin*

Garnett, Chris Paul, Marc Gasol, Yao Ming, Al Horford, Amar'e Stoudemire, DeMar DeRozan, Isaiah Thomas, Kemba Walker and Chris Bosh in the Kindle Store. If you love basketball, check out my website at claytongeoffreys.com to join my exclusive list where I let you know about my latest books and give you lots of goodies.

Like what you read? Please leave a review!

I write because I love sharing the stories of influential people like John Wall with fantastic readers like you. My readers inspire me to write more so please do not hesitate to let me know what you thought by leaving a review! If you love books on life, basketball, or productivity, check out my website at claytongeoffreys.com to join my exclusive list where I let you know about my latest books. Aside from being the first to hear about my latest releases, you can also download a free copy of *33 Life Lessons: Success Principles, Career Advice & Habits of Successful People*. See you there!

Clayton

References

[i] "John Wall". *Draft Express*. Web.

[ii] "Analyzing the NBA Combine Measurements". *Draft Express*. 22 May 2010. Web.

[iii] Givony, Jonathan. "NBA Draft Prospect of the Week: John Wall". *Draft Express*. 16 December 2009. Web.

[iv] Prada, Mike. "The Old John Wall Scouting Report is Now Useless". *SB Nation*. 4 May 2015. Web.

[v] Lee, Michael. "John Wall Traces Success in March to Summer Work". *Washington Post*. 26 March 2013. Web.

[vi] Lee, Michael. "John Wall Out Eight Weeks Because of Stress Injury in Right Knee". *Washington Post*. 28 September 2012. Web.

[vii] Khan, Umair. "Examining John Wall's Improved Jump Shot". *SB Nation*. 18 September 2013. Web

[viii] Freeman, Eric. "John Wall Became Wizards Leader When his Teammates Forced Him to Be One". *Ball Don't Lie*. 13 March 2014. Web.

[ix] Baig, Osman. "Washington Wizards' Step Towards The NBA Finals: Wittman and Offensive Improvement". *Fan Sided*. 29 August 2014. Web.

[x] Kennedy, Alex. "NBA PM: John Wall Enters MVP Conversation". *Basketball Insiders*. 17 December 2014. Web.

[xi] Moore, Matt. "Why Wizards' John Wall Faces Most Important Season of His Career". *CBS Sports*. 15 September 2015. Web.

[xii] Castillo, Jorge. "John Wall has Surgery on Both Knees: His Status for Wizards Training Camp is Unknown". *Washington Post*. 5 May 2016. Web.

[xiii] Lee, Albert. "John Wall, Bradley Beal Must Work Through Their Tension for the Wizards to Succeed". *SB Nation*. 23 August 2016. Web.

[xiv] Schultz, Jordan. "John Wall: When I have a Guy One-on-One Guarding Me, I Feel Like He's at My Mercy". *Huffington Post*. 25 February 2015. Web.

[xv] Brewer, Jerry. "The offseason that slowed John Wall down might allow him to go full speed again". *The Washington Post*. 26 October 2016. Web.

[xvi] Spears, Marc J. "John Wall on His Relationship With Bradley Beal and Taking the Washington Wizards All the Way". *The Undefeated*. 15 March 2017.

Made in the USA
Columbia, SC
12 February 2019